Three Economies of Transcendence

Forerunners: Ideas First

Short books of thought-in-process scholarship, where intense analysis, questioning, and speculation take the lead

FROM THE UNIVERSITY OF MINNESOTA PRESS

Dominic Boyer
No More Fossils

Sharad Chari
Gramsci at Sea

Kathryn J. Gindlesparger
Opening Ceremony: Inviting Inclusion into University Governance

J. Logan Smilges
Crip Negativity

Shiloh Krupar
Health Colonialism: Urban Wastelands and Hospital Frontiers

Antero Garcia
All Through the Town: The School Bus as Educational Technology

Lydia Pyne
Endlings: Fables for the Anthropocene

Margret Grebowicz
Rescue Me: On Dogs and Their Humans

Sabina Vaught, Bryan McKinley Jones Brayboy, and Jeremiah Chin
The School–Prison Trust

After Oil Collective; Ayesha Vemuri and Darin Barney, Editors
Solarities: Seeking Energy Justice

Arnaud Gerspacher
The Owls Are Not What They Seem: Artist as Ethologist

Tyson E. Lewis and Peter B. Hyland
Studious Drift: Movements and Protocols for a Postdigital Education

Mick Smith and Jason Young
Does the Earth Care? Indifference, Providence, and Provisional Ecology

Caterina Albano
Out of Breath: Vulnerability of Air in Contemporary Art

Gregg Lambert
The World Is Gone: Philosophy in Light of the Pandemic

Grant Farred
Only a Black Athlete Can Save Us Now

Anna Watkins Fisher
Safety Orange

(Continued on page 78)

Three Economies of Transcendence

Andrea Righi

University of Minnesota Press

MINNEAPOLIS

LONDON

Portions of chapter 2 appeared in a different form in "The Currency of the Anthropocene: Dismantling the Theological Presupposition of Neoliberalism in Kim Stanley Robinson's *The Ministry for the Future*," *European Journal of Creative Practices and Landscapes* 5, no. 2 (2022): 61–77. Portions of chapter 3 appeared in a different form in "Eternity as Relationality: The Problem of the External Foundation of Time in the Thought of Emanuele Severino," *Journal of Italian Philosophy* 6 (2023): 77–94.

ISBN 978-1-5179-1838-5 (PB)
ISBN 978-1-4529-7216-9 (Ebook)
ISBN 978-1-4529-7367-8 (Manifold)

Published by the University of Minnesota Press, 2025
111 Third Avenue South, Suite 290
Minneapolis, MN 55401-2520
www.upress.umn.edu

Available as a Manifold edition at manifold.umn.edu

The University of Minnesota is an equal-opportunity educator and employer.

To Noah

Contents

Introduction

LACK OF POLITICAL WILL AND CORRUPTION of the ruling class are certainly enormous obstacles but do not (fully) explain the widespread inaction against our current multidimensional crisis (ecological catastrophe, failing democracies, permanent and more destructive wars, etc.). In *We Are the Weather,* Jonathan Safran Foer writes that our ecocidal society faces a veritable crisis of belief: We are aware of the dramatic consequences of our actions and choose to ignore them.[1] This is not simply a cognitive blockage. Although there are many forms of denial, I suspect they have a common origin. On one side, a minority believes that this is a conspiracy or, equally irrationally, knows the effects of global warming but believes that it will be spared. On the other, a majority behaves like Achilles in Zeno's paradox. A collapse is imminent, but the gap between now and then (in fact, an infinite number of instants) allows them to repress the looming disaster and bask in a kind of indefinite present.[2] When looked at closely, the underlining characteristic of these behaviors is that they

1. Jonathan Safran Foer, *We Are the Weather: Saving the Planet Begins at Breakfast* (Farrar, Straus, and Giroux, 2019).
2. Kari-Mari Norgaard calls it *implicatory denial*; see her *Living in Denial: Climate Change, Emotions, and Everyday Life* (MIT Press, 2011).

foreclose the limitedness of our existence, thereby creating an abstract infinity that takes over reality. Consider the increasingly common case of wealthy people investing in big plans to ride out the apocalypse. They firmly support the dogma of infinite accumulation via predation that is responsible for our catastrophe while believing that that very accumulation will save them. The logic of excess of neoliberalism cannot imagine alternatives to itself; rather, it doubles down on its infinite expansion.

To understand why we revere such limitless growth, we need to turn our attention to the symbolic construction of transcendence. In the West, transcendence rules by replacing the here and now of life with the elsewhere of infinite value, a web of injunctions and pressures to augment said value that quashes any urgency to act. While it organized the field of life externally—ruling much like a sovereign by virtue of his exceptionality—transcendence, in fact, originates from an anthropological incongruity of humankind itself.[3] As I will discuss, the human animal is structurally ex-centric, always in excess to herself, a condition that may occasion the adoption of defensive mechanisms. Hence, although ex-centricity is inherent to human life and evolution, the response to this instability produces transcendent institutions (i.e., the *Other*) that offer refuge, binding anxiety through the assurance of protection. To use a Feuerbachian language, insofar as the infinity of human life is alienated, it generates a superior universal infinity that fulfills this very function. From this repression, transcendence emerges as a tripartite power that disciplines our modes of life. They are an economy of rank, an economy of infinite valorization, and a phallic economy of time.

---

3. See Andrea Righi, "Sexed Transcendentals: Reading Giorgio Agamben Through the Supplement of Sexual Difference," *Diacritics* 47, no. 2 (2019): 22–47.

The complex interplay of these functions shapes the fundamental dimensions of subjectivity, society, and time, respectively.

In this book, I analyze these structures and propose for each a countermodel, namely, an economy of noncoincidence, an economy of social infinity, and an economy of eternity. The interaction of these countermodels offers tools to breach the systems of control emanating from transcendence and may help us to reactivate the potentials for a different future. Before I begin my analysis, however, I want to make a point about my approach. Just like any critic of Feuerbach's "projection theory" claims, atheism quickly turns into a new religion by substituting a God-Man with the belief in a Man-God.[4] In other words, declaring the oppressive and false nature of transcendence—that is to say, stating that immanence is all that exists—risks replacing this metaphysical position with a new transcendence. This assertion would entail naming a new foundation, thus incurring in the same shortfalls of an elsewhere that gives cohesion to the field as in the formalism established by transcendence itself. By contrast, the radical immanence that I seek to outline as an alternative to the three economies of transcendence cannot be directly affirmed but rather should emerge from the internal dissolution of transcendence itself. Similarly, the solutions to our crisis must grow out of the terminal spasms of the current order. It is thus necessary to enter into a strange relation with transcendence and take up its material and anthropological genesis as if it were true to let them implode internally.[5] What emerges from the dissolution

---

4. Jacek Uglik, "Ludwig Feuerbach's Conception of the Religious Alienation of Man and Mikhail Bakunin's Philosophy of Negation," *Studies in East European Thought* 62, no. 1 (2010): 23.

5. See Aristides Baltas, *Peeling Potatoes or Grinding Lenses: Spinoza and Young Wittgenstein Converse on Immanence and Its Logic* (University of Pittsburgh Press, 2012).

of transcendence is the gleam of an immanent scene, one that is (self)-organized via the primary role of relationality and its ecopolitical implications. This is the methodology I follow as I interrogate authors like René Girard and Paolo Virno (part 1) to articulate a different ecology of the relationship with the other or discuss the misunderstood meaning of money by comparing it to a new green digital currency in Kim Stanley Robinson's novel *The Ministry for the Future* (part 2). Correspondingly, in part 3, I establish a dialogue between Hannah Arendt, Adriana Cavarero, and Emanuele Severino by gesturing toward a sense of time that is based not on a sense of death but on life and persistence.

1. The Economy of Rank

TO THE EXTENT THAT AN ECONOMY, as Aaron Schuster writes, is "a strategy for handling the trouble of desire, and instituting a manageable relation to the other," neoliberalism's most successful operation is to enact an economy of desire through a form of secularized transcendence.[1] While the transcendent God of Christianity presided upon the judgment of mortals, the new Other of neoliberalism simply commands the growth of value. Presently, transcendence is an abstract formula of incessant valorization that idiotically wants "more." It thus establishes a model of desire through metrics of success, sometimes called benchmarking, that are effective in shaping environments where individuals live in a competition that depletes their existence, a process that is specular to the global destruction of our planet.[2] I call this an economy of rank, or distinction, because it is based on antagonistic relations with others as well as with oneself—the neoliberal mantra "reach your full potential" is simply a form

1. Aaron Schuster, "The Debt Drive: Philosophical Anthropology and Political Economy," YouTube video, https://youtu.be /Pno5X5AV0UM.
2. See Andrea Righi, *The Other Side of the Digital: The Sacrificial Economy of New Media* (University of Minnesota Press, 2021).

of accountability to the always-more logic of transcendence. One finds a remarkable finalism at the root of this economy that frames the drive to eminence as necessary for progress.

PayPal founder and adviser to President Donald Trump Peter Thiel claims that "even if climate change is quite as bad as people think it is, if we group think we're more likely to misdiagnose the problem."[3] Setting aside the incongruity of Thiel's argument—apparently the ideological conformism of neoliberalism is not a problem—let us pause on how he conceives of difference only in terms of superiority. The highest value resides in breaking away from the sameness of groupthink. Difference is merely a sign of separation from others—a rather nonspecific element that, however, becomes the driver of progress because it is considered an invariant trait of humanity. In these pages, I expose the contextual and phallic essence of an economy of rank while also pointing out an alternative economy of noncoincidence that foregrounds the role of alterity for the self and its relationships with others.

Difference as a Product of Rivalry

French theoretician René Girard was an intellectual mentor to Peter Thiel. Although Hobbesian inflected, Girard's analysis of rivalry and imitation remains far more innovative than Thiel's reductionist critique of conformism. Girard's initial assumption is simple: Uniformity is a quasi-natural condition for humanity, while difference is the driving force at an individual level. Difference should not be thought of as an externality, something that is discovered and appropriated; rather, it is a product of an internal process that generates differentiation through the asser-

3. James Osborne, "Climate Change Doubt Voiced," *Houston Chronicle,* March 8, 2017.

tion of the superiority of one individual over the rest. Difference depends on the human ambition to outrank others and the social effect that such distinction produces—the hero always needs a public. The public nature of rank has, thus, two consequences. First, because difference is produced internally via differentiation, its corresponding dimension—that is, transcendence— is marked not by unconditionality but rather by its immanent origins. However, recognizing the internal, humanlike quality of transcendence, Girard also declares its universality, thus reintroducing the same essentialist logic he previously critiqued. As we will see, far from being a general law, Girard's analysis is, in fact, useful for understanding the economic theology that dominates the phallic drive of neoliberalism. Second, to the extent that power needs the powerless to sustain its superiority, any rank economy must rely on a network of interdependencies based on the nature of desire—a condition that limits this type of domination more than commonly thought. For Girard, desire is never individual, nor is a direct assertion of one's will. It is, rather, a vicarious volition that obeys a model. As social beings, humans learn desire through the example of others, and this modeling capacity does not vanish in time. Desire is not authentic, nor is it ultimately an individual choice; it is always the desire of and by the Other. The Other can be a real person but it is usually an imagined entity that shapes and orients passions.[4] This is why, for Girard, desire is fundamentally derivative and thus mimetic. But the fact that we desire what the Other desires also suggests that

4. Although Girard does not discuss it, Jacques Lacan had already given a full and more balanced expression to this notion, which he formulated on the backbone of phenomenology—the conclusion (a veritable theorem) being that "the gaze I encounter is not a seen gaze, but a gaze imagined by me in the field of the Other." Lacan, *On Feminine Sexuality, the Limits of Love and Knowledge, 1972–1973* (W. W. Norton, 1999), 81.

our wants are largely "undifferentiated," or homologized, as he notes.[5] In effect, Girardian subjectivity doesn't desire anything in particular, or rather, it wants something specific only insofar as it allows the subject to achieve prominence. The goal is to occupy a symbolic position. However, because it is a matter of status, the object of desire is paradoxical. On one side, to the extent that it is coveted by everybody, it is a dull, homologizing object. On the other, because it signals real difference, the object produces a form of absolute uniqueness and is literally exceptional. Strictly speaking, the modeling capacity of desire generates a mirror effect that drives individuals to seek conformity under the guidance of uniqueness.

When applied to situations in which issues of prestige, honor, and status are significant, Girard's theoretical model is quite effective. Consider the opening canto of Matteo Boiardo's famous epic poem *L'Orlando innamorato* (1483), in which Angelica, the beautiful daughter of the king of Cathay, makes a consequential appearance at the court of Charlemagne. Boiardo writes that each Christian and Muslim lord is "won by her beauty, stunned by the sight."[6] The imitative force of desire casts a spell on the court, obscuring the individuality of these heroes, nearly blurring the difference between Christian and Muslim. Their wives are similarly flattened, relegated to an aesthetic mediocrity in comparison to Angelica. Angelica's grand entrance reflects her status as a prize and coveted object—as well as the secret weapon of the Muslim army; the Carolingian knights are, in fact, drawn into a clash to win her over, and instead of closing ranks, they

5. René Girard, *To Double Business Bound* (Johns Hopkins University Press, 1978), 91.

6. Matteo Maria Boiardo, *L'Orlando innamorato* (Poetry in Translation, 2022), https://www.poetryintranslation.com/PITBR/Italian/BoiardoBookICantoI.php#anchor_Toc90806517.

compete to demonstrate their honor. Boiardo's ironic perspective should not be overlooked. Still, Angelica perfectly represents the paradoxical nature of the object of desire. For these knights, she is both a homogenizing and a unique, or scarce, object. Similarly, because that which is desirable is reduced to the idea of prey, she is both elevated and othered. Girard's analysis rarely questions the status of the desirable, which, insofar as it is codified as a property (and cannot assume a positive, independent valence), is usually feminine.

It is in the nature of the desirable to inevitably stir up competition. The winner, in fact, acts as a pole of attraction for other members. This overdetermination of (masculine) passions follows a triangular structure that unifies the group through the sameness of their perception and libidinal investments. According to Girard, "desiring mimesis engenders its objects, but nevertheless it always appears to the outside observer as a triangular configuration the angles of which are occupied respectively by the two rivals and their common object. The object always comes to the foreground and mimesis is hidden behind it, even in the eyes of the desiring subjects. The convergence of desire defines the object."[7] The object is a decoy. What matters is the relation about the competing males, who sustain and reproduce a mimetic model via a compounded effect. Through mutual reinforcement, rivalry increases the value of the object in question. This means that Angelica's beauty is accrued because Charlemagne's best knight, Orlando, falls in love with her. Similarly, Orlando's infatuation must be equally deserving because all other Christian and Muslim knights want her as well. The paradoxical nature of mimetic antagonism points to a typical Girardian loop where it is impossible to distinguish between

---

7. Girard, *To Double Business Bound,* 91.

cause and effect. What exactly causes Angelica's desirability is hard to say: Is it purely Angelica's beauty, or is it Orlando's desire and its effects on the knights? Similarly, is it Angelica or the knights' awe that fuels Orlando's passion?

This endless loop of desire is the matrix for another equally infinite loop: violence. As observed, Angelica stands for a totality that only one person will enjoy. Such conquest, however, does not put an end to the competition because the prestige of the desirable object draws its force precisely from the intensity of admiration and the envy it generates. These feelings all but ensure the continuation of a series of conflicts. This is why Girard writes that "he who has struck the last blow rises above the other," boasting his "mystic prize as long as he can believe his triumph is definitive, as long as his adversary does not steal it back."[8] Consider the paradoxes we just mentioned: an object that is both homogenizing and scarce; competitors who validate and augment each other's standing despite a hierarchy; and finally, the lack of a cause for said animosity, for Girard observes that "it is truly impossible to fix the origin of and responsibility for the rivalry, whose inexhaustible source is mimesis."[9] The most striking consequence for a model based on difference is that mimesis itself breeds a generalized indistinction. To the extent that the desire of the Other determines the desirable, it is hard to point out the specificity of the object of such desire and, likewise, to attribute the roles of the imitated and imitators. The template of mimetic desire is based on interdependent circuits that feed on themselves. Under these circumstances, mimesis is a self-organized symbolic system managing those who (usually men) are caught in it.

8. Girard, 94.
9. Girard, 91.

The Sacrificial Violence of Religion

According to Girard, the complex of mimetic desire transcends the individual level. Functioning as an anthropological law, it actually explains the origin of religions. From his standpoint, the divine beyond is inextricably bound with mimesis as the invariant principle that enables hominization. As the hostility emanating from mimesis leads to a cycle of vendettas that brings the group to the brink of civil war, religion mitigates these endemic crises through a set of sacrificial mechanisms aimed at ensuring stability against intragroup fighting. In this sense, scapegoating is the solution to containing warfare and the result of basic psychological group dynamics. It is an unconscious and self-reinforcing mechanism that brings peace by sacrificing a designated victim. Nikolaus Wandinger summarizes this mechanism as follows: "Upon experiencing this sudden and unexpected peace, the group 'realizes' that the culprit they had just killed was not an ordinary criminal. He/she was so powerful that his/her death catapulted their society from destructive, all-out war to harmonious peace. . . . The villain was not just a villain but a god/dess capable of both destroying and saving. The reality of this deity is confirmed by the very power of the experiences he/she provoked."[10] Once a group embraces this social arrangement, it will inevitably codify it via rituals and sacraments. In religion, violence becomes structural; in other words, it is validated and institutionally motivated. A mob lynching a designated victim is the crude solution that religion refines by establishing a complex system of rituals through which aggressions are orderly doled out. As the tech-

10. Nikolaus Wandinger, "Religion and Violence: A Girardian Overview," *Journal of Religion and Violence* 1, no. 2 (2013): 130.

nology devised to manage crises, sacrifice is a form of "good violence" that humans enact to avoid the abyss of civil war, what
the Greeks called *stasis*.[11] But as the cycle of blood is always
on the verge of beginning again, more culprits are required to
produce a difference that channels intra-aggression toward the
outside. Humans make the sacred via the spilling of blood, and
the idea that the gods want a sacrifice enables them to "dispose
of their violence more efficiently," because, Girard explains,
"they regard the process not as something emanating from
within themselves, but as a necessity imposed from without,
a divine decree whose least infraction calls down terrible punishment."[12] Violence is a pragmatic mechanism aimed at human
well-being, one that is ordered and legitimated from above.

The specularity between the sacrificial and mimetic desire
is blatant. Like the object of desire, the scapegoat acts as the
recipient of emotional intensities, thus producing the difference
needed to counteract homogeneity. Here, too, difference is the
structural mechanism that is produced and consumed because of
(masculine) homogeneity. What's more, the scapegoat points to
an ambivalent symbolic position. Behind gods, heroes, and kings
stands the lynched victim, who becomes the culprit of societies'
ills, just as behind the object of desire stands a subject who is
adored insofar as she is turned into a mute ideality. Finally, as
the victim's execution appeases fractures and divisions, it also
forecasts an external point of difference, an externality that so-
lidifies transcendence. As Girard writes, "transcendence is, in
short, only because it serves as a deceiving object of rivalry."[13] In

11. René Girard, *Violence and the Sacred* (Johns Hopkins University
Press, 1979), 37.

12. Girard, 14.

13. Girard, *To Double Business Bound,* 111.

this civilizing process, transcendence sanctions the difference groups produce while killing sacrificial victims.

For Girard, this social engineering is effective only insofar as it remains hidden. Once the apparatus is revealed, its efficacy vanishes. Only the Judeo-Christian world unveils the truth of this brutality, for as Wandinger writes, the biblical revelation rests on "the insight that God is not siding with the multitude that convenes on a single victim, but that God is a protector of victims, and underdogs."[14] The Christian revelation is not void of a series of difficulties and equivocations. Girard acknowledges the presence of an extensive sacrificial economy in the history of Christianism that he characterizes as a deviation from the original message, a relapse into previous violent practices due to the concept of blood in the Epistle to the Hebrews (Hebrews 9:22–26)—an understanding of blood that redeems sin because of the crucifixion of Jesus. Even though present-day Catholic doctrine continues to profess the salvific meaning of the crucifixion, Girard contends that what was once "acceptable to the medieval mind" has now "become intolerable to us."[15] What is intolerable is the reintroduction of the tributary pact between people and God—one in which the scapegoat represents the price for our well-being. The crucifixion, in fact, does not perpetuate but interrupts the sacrificial machine by dissolving violent mimesis and the contractual force that binds a community through blood spilling.

By negating redemption via sacrifice, and thus violence, Christianity exposes the essence of the divine and simultaneously marks a radical departure from it. Specifically, Christianism roots itself in the fundamental anthropogenetic mechanism of sacrifice

14. Wandinger, "Religion and Violence," 132.
15. René Girard, *Things Hidden Since the Foundation of the World* (Stanford University Press, 1987), 182.

while simultaneously terminating it.[16] For archaic religions, the scapegoat is always guilty in the eyes of the community—in this sense, Oedipus is expelled by the Thebans to rid the city of the Plague. Going against a redemptive quid pro quo, however, Jesus takes upon himself the debt of society because he is innocent. The crucifixion does not offer the cleansing of sins in exchange for Jesus's blood; rather, it offers something more miraculous: the revelation that mimetic violence does not produce the divine. This is perhaps also the true meaning of redemption: freedom from the sacrificial economy. Once the good news is uttered, however, all we have is this life on earth. Girard glosses, "So now we are liberated. We know that we are by ourselves, with no father in the sky to punish us and interfere with our paltry business. So we must no longer look backward but forward; we must show what man is capable of."[17]

The true divinity of God resides not in transcendence but in the message that exposes and severs the bond with violence and dependence. Yet, transcendence is not abolished; rather, it transitions from the needed but negative case of the scapegoat to the positive but exclusive one of the Christian revelation. In other words, the crucifixion is a discontinuity so radical that it stands out as a point of (positive) transcendence. This revelation breaks away from the very idea of the economy that has ruled (at least according to Girard) humanity since time immemorial, one in which desire is subjected to a contractual logic priced in blood.

It goes without saying that the effects of this new economy have been remarkably insignificant in our history, particular-

16. The good news of the Gospels rests on the idea that "they avoided sacralizing the victim as the guilty party and prevented him [Jesus] from being held responsible for the purely human disorders that his death was supposed to end." Girard, 194.

17. Girard, 195.

ly when one considers the Crusades, the Inquisition, and the endless persecution of a variety of peoples, not to mention the infinite series of wars sponsored or fought by Christianity. Girard perhaps gestures toward this legacy, but deviation from historical truth is not the problem here.[18] The problem is the transcendent paradigm at work even in the solution. Girard calls it transcendent love, which is based on "the act of destroying those [mimetic] powers through a form of transcendence that never acts by means of violence."[19] This is the definition of God for Girard, and "this is indeed why the Son promises men that if they manage to behave as the Father wishes, and to do his will, they will all become sons of God," because "it is not God who sets up the barriers between himself and mankind, but mankind himself."[20] Still, the persistence of a philosophy marked by transcendence prevents Girard from recognizing the alternatives available to desire and politics. The only two existing options are to follow the dominating direction of rivalry or to negate it altogether. One must be a realist and acknowledge the reality of violence or be a saint and abolish it. The final prize, the highest value, can be reached only through a purely voluntaristic action.[21] Not surprisingly, the content of Jesus's exception evaporates quickly. In right-wing intellectual circles, what remains is its empty, voluntaristic form and the thrill of the discovery of mimetic rivalry

18. Girard writes that the misunderstanding of the true meaning of the passion induces Christianity to "re-establish cultural forms which remain sacrificial, . . . still clinging to the sacrificial vision that the Gospels rejects" (181).

19. Girard, 214.

20. Girard, 215.

21. The male imaginary constructs itself as self-sufficient and self-positing because it interdicts the symbolic dimension of the mother. See Righi, *Other Side of the Digital,* 3–7.

resulting in difference. Girard himself carves out a special case of rivalry without violence as he celebrates capitalism, a system that is productive because it "ritualizes and institutionalizes mimetic rivalry, the rules of which are willingly obeyed."[22] Likewise, the neoliberal elite that ruled over the last thirty years of globalization equates the condition of sameness to any form of social intervention, while it magnifies the true difference produced by the healthy competition of the so-called free market. As observed, neoliberalism fuels phallic forms of desire through an economy of rank in which transcendence operates as a driver of the expansion of surplus value. The fantasized Other of neoliberalism demands said growth; the elsewhere of pure value is the device that enables such economic theology.

This symbolic system not only has nefarious consequences for the health of the planet but also enables a widespread inertia regarding climate action. For those who deny the effects of global warming, it guarantees that natural resources are indeed infinite. For those who accept them, this model activates the mechanism of salvation. Any apocalypse holds the promise of spiritual (or physical) deliverance for true believers. Whether or not the world goes up in flame or is flooded, some people will be saved. For the rest of the world that is concerned, transcendence allows the temporary repression of the immediacy of the crisis. Because infinity is projected onto the domain of the elsewhere, it acquires a mystical quality that contaminates life in general, turning it into an endless present that dulls the gravity of our situation. Such repression generates, in turn, a widespread eco-anxiety that struggles to take a concrete form. The thought of immanence, instead, looks at our human condition and the natural

22. René Girard, "Innovation and Repetition," *Substance* 19, no. 62/63 (1990): 17. He also bashes the counterculture of 1968 for having waged a war against the sanctity of imitation (17).

limits it encounters to seek out the possibility for transformation in the here and now of our condition. These futurities must be embryonic in the present; otherwise, they are mere idealities. Naturally, this inquiry must take into account anthropological invariants as well, but it is necessary to avoid a modeling that is as reductionist as mimetic rivalry.

Friendship and the Economy of Noncoincidence

In the economy of rank, transcendence operates both as an imperative to dominate others via the possession of the desired object and as an injunction to preserve the group via the othering of a sacrificial victim. By reducing virtually all human interactions to this model, Girard's mimetic theory of desire constructs human evolution as a finalistic and phallic enterprise. Feminism convincedly made this point early on when Girard's theory was gaining traction in the 1980s. Toril Moi argued that Girard was merely reiterating "Luce Irigaray's reading of sexual relations under patriarchy."[23] On one side, Girard discovers the modeling and impersonal capacity of desire. On the other, as Moi notes, he "assumes that heterosexuality is prescribed by our instinctual apparatus inherited from animal life, that is to say that the object-choice is instinctually given."[24] This dominating preference for the phallic is indisputable only for a warrior aristocracy or in any environment where the drive to prominence is achieved through spectacles of competition, prevarication, and dominance.

Far from being universal, mimetic theory seems to overlook the many instances in which society manages desire without

23. Toril Moi, "The Missing Mother: The Oedipal Rivalries of René Girard," *Diacritics* 12 (1982): 29.

24. Moi, 29.

privileging antagonism.[25] Robert Pfaller, for instance, elaborated the concept of surrogate enjoyment or "interpassivity," which studies how delegating pleasure to somebody else turns into a source of pleasure in itself.[26] Interpassivity may create hierarchies; however, it is less subject centered and thus more inclined to convivial behavior. Furthermore, rituals are not only tributary pledges to transcendence but also self-contained acts that soften the difference between devotees and a God that is set apart from them. An example of such immanent practices is Émile Durkheim's interpretation of the Feast of the Tabernacles, in which the rhythmic movement of willow branches "mechanically produce[s] the effects which are the reason for their existence," namely, the wind that brings rain and, eventually, a bountiful harvest.[27]

If one concedes that because of mimesis our interactions are ultimately based on some symbolic authority, one should also admit that this authority, just like any other social element, may take shapes that are different from an economy of rank. This is all the more true because mimesis has a much ampler meaning than

25. Slavoj Žižek argues that the dominant tonality of neoliberal society is one that, however, does not believe and yet still acts in a certain way. See Žižek, "Believe It or Not," *Drawbridge,* no. 1 (2006). The possibility of disavowal undermines the power of revelation precisely by undoing the effects of truth that Girard cherishes so much. The problem here is not only the long-standing misunderstanding of Jesus's message but also the possibility that people perfectly understood it and nonetheless decided to follow the violent authority of the mythical world.

26. Robert Pfaller, *Interpassivity: The Aesthetics of Delegated Enjoyment* (Edinburgh University Press, 2017), 8.

27. Émile Durkheim, *Elementary Forms of the Religious Life* (Macmillan, 1915), 34. Similarly, studying tarantism, the anthropologist Ernesto De Martino illustrated the use of musical practices aimed at reintegrating presence into the life of peasant society. See De Martino, *The Land of Remorse* (Free Association Books, 2005).

Girard's definition in biology, even in the case of hominization. Roberto Marchesini maintains that the human animal is fully immersed in "zoo-mimesis," a primal function that contributed to its definition as a species.[28] By observing and feeling like a bird, for instance, a plethora of possibilities manifested in early humans, including perhaps a different, aerial understanding of space. But by mimicking other entities, humans also introjected otherness, thus producing a hybrid identity. This structural hybridity decenters humankind, making it *ex-centric* to itself and its environment, a common feature in the biological world. As Marchesini explains, eccentricity "is not a starting condition proper to the human nature; rather, it is the outcome of a mimetic process," one that involves encounter and socializing with other nonhuman animals, organic and inorganic alterities.[29]

This definition of mimesis helps us move from an economy of rank that dominates neoliberalism to an alternative economy of noncoincidence that, although present in our societies, is buried under a series of misconceptions. In this sense, Paolo Virno's theory of human development does not restrict the breadth of options available to a sacrificial and extractivist logic; rather, it embraces the ex-centric dimension of the human by combining with Vittorio Gallese's mirror neurons theory. Mirror neurons theory argues that the social nature of our life-form is grounded

28. Roberto Marchesini, *Over the Human: Post-Humanism and the Concept of Animal Epiphany* (Springer, 2017), 109–13.

29. Marchesini, 107. Eccentricity, Marchesini concludes, produces hominization precisely "when the human phylogenetic body melts to give life to a symbolic hybrid body that transcends the former because it has been infected with the predicates of difference" (107). Paolo Virno uses instead a notion of eccentricity borrowed from Helmut Plessner that is highly problematic because it devalues animals by reducing them to entities overdetermined by their environment. My analysis deliberately diverges from Virno's Plessnerian paradigm.

in the phylogenetic chain of evolution of our sensorial organs and brain. This approach reverses the classic model of the mind, which begins from an individual who is combined with others, thus producing society. In contrast, "the mind of an individual is the product of a process of differentiation that takes place in the collective praxis."[30] Gallese calls this dimension the *we-centric-space,* a "tight relationship between human sociality and the natural and intrinsic pragmatic relatedness we entertain with the world, on the one hand, and our constitutive—ontological—relatedness to others."[31] Difference is the hybridization process that emerges in the we-centric-space, a form of effervescence integral to relationality, not the distinction of one individual over the others.

Superimposed on this intersubjective dimension, we find language. Virno argues that language does not "limit itself to embellishing and refining the we-centric-space already delineated by mirror neurons"; rather, it "destructively retroacts on this space, undermining its solidity."[32] In other words, the mimetic predisposition that informs the infrastructure of our animality is dilatated, bended, and pierced by language. Negation, in particular, illustrates how language complicates the we-centric space. When negating a fact, we are actually affirming that initial identity in order to turn it around. He writes that "the distinctive trait of linguistic negation . . . amounts to proposing again one and the same semantic content with an opposite algebraic sign."[33] For instance, by saying that a refugee is not really like us, I am

30. Paolo Virno, *An Essay on Negation: For a Linguistic Anthropology* (Seagull Books, 2018), 7 (modified).

31. Vittorio Gallese, "The Two Sides of Mimesis: Mimetic Theory, Embodied Simulation, and Social Identification," in *Mimesis and Science* (Michigan State University Press, 2011), 91.

32. Virno, *An Essay on Negation,* 11.

33. Virno, 13.

asserting two things at once: that this refugee is a person but that, as a refugee, he is also something else—a criminal, perhaps; hence I can let him die without regret. Negation is always supplementary; the negative sign shifts the value of an entity once it has been acknowledged. This capacity for active misrecognition illustrates a mechanism common in the biological realm, which the human, however, has magnified to a remarkable level of complexity: the potentiality both for recognition (mimesis) and for full-fledged misrecognition (negation) that produces a deviation from reality. This is a double-edged sword. Because "non-recognition is grounded . . . on the tendency of the sign 'not' to evoke a difference that . . . is at each turn accounted for through some contingent property," it may open unexpected solutions that imaginatively break with what looks like an unavoidable direction, or it may produce endless conflict.[34] In the case of conflict, negation is very powerful. By not recognizing reality, it unleashes a form of destructive violence that is unparalleled in other animals.

Yet, negation may also act to mitigate its original violence. Virno indicates the public sphere as a form of second-degree negation. The public sphere "has the form of a negation of negation. It is a *not* that is added before the phrase non-man," thus quashing the mechanical liquidation that the misrecognition of another human being inevitably generates.[35] The negation of the negation is the correcting mechanism that laboriously recuperates our biological conviviality. Yet, this recuperation is not immediate, nor is it a simple re-presentation. If the we-centric-space is the "infallible and impersonal neural co-feeling," the public sphere is the struggle for "persuasion, the metamorphosis and crisis of

34. Virno, 18.
35. Virno, 19.

the process of production, the brutality of political conflicts."[36] Virno does not idealize the public sphere. Just as in the case of the first-degree negation, the public sphere opens up a set of determinations that can be beneficial but also detrimental to the human community. Following Girard's examination of religion, one can easily see how sacrificial rites work as a negation of a negation without actually moving away from the original, violent misrecognition. As a public, institutionalized practice—as I discussed earlier—sacrifice allows a selective violence to be executed as a duty. A careful assessment of what goals and rules politics enacts is key to avoiding the terrible consequences of negation, because, Virno writes, "institutions offer real protection only to the extent that they make use of those very conditions that, under different circumstances, continuously produce a threat."[37]

When organized toward emancipative and collective goals, these institutions make good use of human negation by exhibiting their rootedness in their immanent substratum—let us remark in passing that this is a sign of the fading away of transcendence. Virno insists on using a "non-dialectical understanding of the negative," which avoids subsuming its noncoincidence via a higher form of unity.[38] The anthropogenic force of negation should not be reduced to the idea of an essential benevolence of humanity (naively adopted by the progressive wing of neoliberalism) nor one of absolute evil (as in the antimodernist and authoritarian wing of reactionary neoliberalism). The capacity for a structural detachment from the reality of the environment and ourselves is all we really are or "have," as I explain later, and that difference emerges in the uses we make of it or in the

36. Virno, 20.

37. Paolo Virno, *E così via, all'infinito: Logica e antropologia* (Bollati Boringhieri, 2010), 159.

38. Virno, 159.

types of protection we choose. To recapitulate our use of mimesis, the natural substratum of the human animal is marked by imitation as a condition of possibility for intersubjectivity and relatedness with alterity. Language retroacts on that hybrid substratum, opening a rift that leads to positive and negative consequences. Negation, as in the proposition "This is not a human being," engenders and supports violence but can also block it by directing it toward forms of conviviality. Negation functions as a differentiating process producing various kinds of differences, not just the difference of superiority, as in the economy of rank.

But what about difference in the singular: the object of desire that guarantees a symbolic position of distinction? What about Girard's idea of the scapegoat, the othering that breaks the sameness of the human group but also ensures its cohesiveness via sacrifice? To respond to this question, we need to look at a recent work by Virno titled *Avere: Sulla natura dell'animale loquace* (2020), in which his analysis of the grammar of the verb *to have* will help us to delineate a positive notion of alterity. In capitalist society, this verb is distorted by the idea of absolute possession, in other words, by the frictionless domination of the object. Any object is thus turned into a thing, something inert, manipulable, acquisitive, and exchangeable. Yet, one could argue that this understanding of the verb is confused with its opposite, the verb *to be*. When we say that we *have* something, it is as if that thing becomes our appendage—what we instead rarely admit is that we may become an appendage of that thing as well. (This is the case with digital technology: Advertised as a tool to empower consumers, it works as a generator of cognitive and emotional pressures that dominate the user.)

The classic Aristotelian definition of humankind as an animal that is endowed with or "has" language shows how the verb *to have* does not reflect possession or control over the object in question; rather, "to have language" signals a lack of adherence, an unfulfillable cohabitation with the linguistic dimension. We are constantly aware of the opaqueness and intractability of the linguistic object; thus we can say that we make *experience* of language, to use Giorgio Agamben's terminology. Likewise, we can say that we have a body, not in the sense that one's self (or soul) pilots a set of organs; rather, the body is that corporeal other that makes one who one is. We are that non-completely-corresponding relationship with the body as other. In this case, Virno recuperates Émile Benveniste's analysis of the verb *to be,* which implies an intrinsic relationship between two substances based on identity, as different from *to have,* which explicitly expresses an extrinsic relation of nonidentity between the two substances. The verb *to have* elucidates this primary detachment that allows us to be what we are as we inhabit our corporeal dimension.

The noncoincidence with language, and, likewise, the hybridity of the human being fomented by mimesis (another form of noncoincidence as nonidentity), is akin to what Virno calls the "singular and fragile whole" of friendship.[39] The grammar of friendship is one that signals no-adherence and illustrates an alternative economy of noncoincidence. Just like the grammar of *to have* indicates a relation between a subject and something else and not a possession, friendship names the moment in which an unsaturable break in anthropological life is brought into relief. A friend is not a twin soul but rather the opposite: In friendship resonates the alterity that already inhabits us. Friendship names the emergence of something that is not familiar.[40] A friend is

39. Paolo Virno, *Avere: Sulla natura dell'animale loquace* (Bollati Boringhieri, 2020), 79.
40. Virno here is drawing on Aristotle's definition of a friend as somebody who is by definition an other *(xenos)*. A friend comes not from the household but from outside.

somebody we might have because friendship illustrates the difference that we embody and enjoy. According to Virno, "noncoincidence" is the existential trait that we enjoy in a friend. This difference is precisely the zone of nonadherence that informs our relationship with language as well as the relationships we have with our bodies.

Admittedly, a politics of friendship has serious limitations when adopted as a political agenda. But Virno's analysis of friendship uncovers a relation to alterity that may help us overcome the limits of the Girardian system. The sacrificial machine throws blame and hatred onto one person, the scapegoat, who is also the twin double of the enemy. Here Girard seems to replicate a superficial definition of friend versus enemy that Carl Schmitt himself at times slipped into, where friends are those who share the same rival. In this sense, it is the common opponent that creates cohesiveness in a group. Virno, however, argues that in Schmitt's thought, the enemy is essentially a concept that is grounded in sovereignty and state power. The true antagonist is a set of "collective subjects who fight over the monopoly of decision of the State."[41] Hence the friend is not the opposite of the enemy because "friendship has no points of contact with state sovereignty," not because it is a private affair but because it belongs to those ontological conditions that make human existence possible.[42]

What must be grasped is that friendship, as an ontological category, allows us to make experience of the constitutional difference that we embody as speaking animals. Virno writes that "in order for the human animal to encounter another itself *(hetero autos),* it is essential that it not fully identify with its salient prerogatives [language]. It is necessary that this animal

41. Virno, 55.
42. Virno, 57.

have, and won't be, a body . . . with a predisposition for speech."[43] Though our biological ex-centricity enables amicable relationships, such otherness is not the sole reason for friendship, else we should all be friends—we all have the ontological disconnect that Virno links to friendship. Noncoincidence resonates in the encounter with the other because it gives birth to the expression of a particular approach to the nonidentity with oneself. To express this affinity, Virno employs the term *style*. Friendship is based on a stylistic mode of expression—a reliable praxis, in other words, an idiosyncratic bridge that keeps friends in a virtuous, interpersonal dialogue. Virno calls this a phatic, performative, and usually gamelike dimension, for "no community of *philoi* exists without famous sentences that liturgically renew the initial connection of votive formulas."[44] Friends are the practitioners of new idiolects that articulate a certain way of inhabiting each other's otherness.[45]

When looking at friendship from the point of view of noncoincidence, we gain access to an idea of the other that differs from the fantastic entity that models and unifies desire via mimetic rivalry—it bears noting that Virno considers issues like envy, as well as honor, betrayal, and shame, as part of friendship. The irreducibility of alterity is a fracture that springs from the self to the bond between individuals. This fracture becomes the gravitational force that fuels the encounter and the process of growth of friendship modulated by a specific flagrance or style,

43. Virno, 57–58.

44. Virno, 81.

45. Virno does not discuss the first induction to difference that happens on the maternal continuum. Although the otherness that the child begins to articulate through his relationship with the mother (or whoever occupies that position) and language is a structural element, it is true that this otherness finds a new degree of introspection when the child develops relationships outside the family.

as observed. The significance of the role played by otherness emerges precisely at the end of a friendship. What happens in these unfortunate cases? Virno notes that when the noncoincidence of the alterity that inhabits us vanishes, friendship ends too. Here the verb *to be* domesticates the intractability of the verb to have; what is left is a sterile determination: My friend is selfish, conservative, and so on. The reduction of friendship to a fixed state liquidates the vitality of the cohabitation with alterity. Thus the indirect and mysterious link with the other that I am is severed and obscured.

The grammar of friendship strikes to the core of a new ecosocial perspective because it illustrates the significance of alterity (ex-centricity) and its modulation (creative expression), thus providing a basic template for a postanthropocentric understanding of nature. What are the implications of having a creek, or even a forest, as a friend? I invite the reader to ponder this question. It would probably entail resisting the idea of considering the environment as something dispensable or that, paternalistically, needs a savior. What's more, it would also push us to welcome a radical alterity and articulate it in unpredictable, hybridized ways. In this respect, an economy of noncoincidence overcomes Girard's depiction of transcendence as a device for the mobilization of a centered subject. With the expression *fuori di sè,* "beyond itself" or ex-centric, Virno indicates a self (an interiority) that grounds its selfness outside its interiority and conversely an exteriority that is contaminated by interiority. This is why Virno redefines transcendence as that domain that "seems situated outside oneself, thus manifesting itself under the guise of detachment and non-identity," and concludes that "transcendence is the *exteriority of what is interior.*"[46] Transcendence is

46. Virno, 183.

the result of noncoincidence and separation because it emerges as an essence that we "have" and thus cannot possess. While transcendence is summarized by the sentence "I have what I am"—which neoliberalism misrepresents as "I own what I am," immanence is expressed by the opposite—"I am what I have."[47] Immanence is the second moment of noncoincidence, when the subject is adroit in those faculties (like style) and "prerogatives that however, remain extrinsic and separated" from it.[48] The economy of rank crumbles once noncoincidence is brought to the foreground. As a unifying principle of rank, transcendence loses its control over the symbolic field because it appears as an illusory projection of a discontinuity, nonidentity, or contradiction. Immanence is the lived-out emanation of that contradiction. It forces us to stare at that abyss without abstraction, such as the invention of a natural infinity capable of absorbing the neoliberal appetite for endless growth or the trick of salvation. In fact, the point of view of noncoincidence finds an application at an economic level, as I discuss in part 2.

47. Virno, 184–85. My understanding of transcendence differs from Virno's.
48. Virno, 185.

2. The Economy of Infinite Valorization

IN PART 1, I pointed out the limits of Girard's theory by sketching an economy of noncoincidence as a possible alternative to the claim that mimesis necessarily produces a will to dominate at the individual level. Today, digital platforms specifically incite mimetic rivalry to generate users' engagement and competition, while, in general, the economy of rank is the symbolic infrastructure that powers much of the extractivist logic responsible for our multifaceted catastrophe. The goal of this chapter is to illustrate and question the ways in which transcendence activates sacrificial mechanisms at a macro level—specifically, at the juncture between theology and economy—that are responsible for the impasse the West faces when tackling global warming.

Western societies display a tendency to imagine the dimension of the absolute—be it power, value, or time—in a beyond-like realm that governs reality from the outside. This symbolic topology creates a landscape of moral and fiscal injunctions. Akin to the deference for the Other exemplified in mimetic rivalry, under this power structure, transcendence captures the social potential of human life via a tributary, sacrificial bond. In other words, transcendence manages the ex-centric nature of humankind by channeling it into an exchange module (or a moral bookkeeping) based on rewards and punishments, in short, a pactional structure that forces individuals to comply with the demands of the Other (God, the King, the Father, etc.). With the term "payability of debt," Eric Santner identifies a narrative that manages the oscillation between lack and excess (our ex-centric condition) by dictating that scarcity can and should always be "made good."[1] This logic emerges at the intersection of theology and economy through the concept of redemption. How the overlap between these two domains absorbs and capitalizes on the social infinity of human relation is the focus of the first section of this part, along with a discussion of the symbolic dimension of money.[2] In the second section, I discuss Kim Stanley Robinson's latest sci-fi novel, *The Ministry for the Future* (2020), to disarm the pactional structure I previously described. To open a pathway for an economy of infinity where transcendence has imploded, I investigate three counternarratives that inform this novel: the new structure of time revealed by the reality of the Anthropocene; a relationship with the other different from that established under a transcendent regime; and, finally, a fully immanent concept of value through a new digital currency that provisions and coordinates people and their institutions.

---

1. Eric Santner, "A Critique of Mana-Theism," posted by Brown University, June 20, 2019, YouTube video, 32:24, https://youtu.be/j4fNKG0JNcY. See also Andrea Righi, "The Pactional Model of Salvation and Its Undoing in Catherine of Siena," *Italian Culture* 40, no. 2 (2022): 112–30.

2. Several scholars have already demonstrated the indistinguishability between the two realms; see Giacomo Todeschini, *Come l'acqua e il sangue* (Carocci, 2021).

The Redemption of Social Infinity

The fusion of the spiritual and the market-like discourses—a veritable "theopolitical economy," according to David Singh—is at the root of the concept of redemption, as the Latin etymology of the verb *red-imere,* in English, "to buy back," discloses.[3] The covenant-making God of the Bible not only strikes down sinners but also accords protection by aiding or saving the lives of his people. In the Old Testament, redemption is notably associated with the rescuing and deliverance of the Jews from slavery and their flight from Egypt. Although in the Hebrew tradition redemption was never exclusively understood as a factual gain, the biblical model for the salvation of the soul as a canceling of material obligations had a long history in antiquity.[4] Leviticus calls for the canceling of material obligations: The Jubilee was the moment in which society would begin again from a clean slate, a common institution in antiquity. Parsing the issue of indebtedness and its relation to widespread enslavement of peasantry at the dawn of large-settled societies, David Graeber observes that "Sumerian and later Babylonian kings periodically announced general amnesties . . . declar[ing] all outstanding consumer debt null and void," thus providing relief and reestablishing social peace within their empires.[5]

3. David Singh, *Divine Currency: The Theological Power of Money in the West* (Stanford University Press, 2018), 12.

4. As Moshe Idel writes, redemption was understood not only as "a material form of retribution" but also as a spiritual and intellectual process whereby "the messianic attainments are related to the impact of the 'divine influx' on the messiah, described also as a divine man." Idel, "Multiple Forms of Redemption in Kabbalah and Hasidism," *Jewish Quarterly Review* 101 (2011): 29, 28.

5. David Graeber, *Debt: The First 5,000 Years* (Melville House, 2012), 65.

Christianity absorbs this basic schema while transforming (or transgressing) it. Its definition of salvation is adopted from Roman law, which referred to the ransom paid by the Senate to entities who held captive Roman soldiers at the time of the Republic. This model rests on the trust that some Other (called *redemptor*) will intervene and on the ensuing tributary relationship between prisoner and benefactor.[6] Therein a contractual or pactional system of reward and punishment emerges as a dominating institution that defines how Christianity envisions redemption in theological terms. This is not the place to show how the accounting of the soul in the afterlife is far from being mathematically sound. However, earthly Christian societies did engage in various forms of redemption by declaring amnesties or adopting systems of welfare for the community. In the Middle Ages, the general tendency to invest in the needs of the *communitas* was called *fructuatio,* while the imperative to donate quotas of capital for good works at the end of one's life fell under the term *restitutio.* Although these mechanisms ensured relief for the community, they were not devoid of a degree of violence—Paul Dumouchel writes that "bonds of solidarity, obligations, and prescriptions restrain the desires of those who have, by imposing upon them a duty to give, and of those who have not, for they must be satisfied with what they get."[7] Giacomo Todeschini points out, for instance, how it was not uncommon for religious authorities like the ninth- to tenth-century century Bishop Ratherius of Verona to claim that the

6. See Tiziana Faitini, "Redimere e riscattare: La redemptio tra teologia e politica," *Politica e Religione: Annuario di Teologia Politica* 16 (2017): 4–6.

7. Paul Dumouchel, *"The Ambivalence of Scarcity" and Other Essays* (University of Michigan Press, 2014), 102.

poor who want riches sin, while the rich, who are unencumbered by wealth, are an example of piety.[8]

Despite social conventions like *fructuatio* and *restitutio,* Christianity progressively liquidates the principles of mutuality that protected community members of what Dumouchel calls "traditional societies" by manipulating transcendence and thus deregulating the contractual system of redemption. Christian theology rewrites the clauses of the Jewish covenant, opening a pathway for dismantling its base of reciprocity. It is no coincidence that one of its targets was the Sabbath year of Leviticus. The spiritualization of the pactional system—one that originates in the understanding of "the infinite value of Christ's body, or of the ecclesiastic community embodied by the Church"—leads to a remarkable repudiation of the Old Testament debt-relief practice.[9] Ecclesiastic authorities like the eleventh-century Benedictine monk Peter Damian made their case against the Jubilee on the basis of a new, unlimited economy of grace. He pointed out that "the precepts of the law are truly fulfilled when they are carried out in accord with the spiritual meaning for which they were instituted. Formerly, while they were being carried out physically, they were empty, that is, a shadow or image of the thing, and not the thing itself."[10] It is the (abstract) infinite dimension of transcendence that shifts the focus from redistribution in this life to the one beyond that. Debt forgiveness in life is only an illusory copy of true forgiveness. By projecting value to

8. See Giacomo Todeschini, *I mercanti e il tempio* (Il Mulino, 2002), 191.

9. Giacomo Todeschini, "The Incivility of Judas," in *Money, Morality, and Culture in Late Medieval and Early Modern Europe* (Routledge, 2016), 38.

10. Peter Damian, *Letters 1–30* (Catholic University of America Press, 1989), 70.

the elsewhere of the divine, Peter Damian discounts earthly salvation. Therein the idealization of infinity supersedes the social infinity of human relations. This transformation of the pactional economy hints at the modulation of transcendence in modern times. As an economic virtue that will be rewarded, neoliberal austerity follows the same sacrificial formalism enacted by the elsewhere of Peter Damian's "thing in itself." Under advanced capitalism, the spiritualization that appreciates the value of the beyond dissolves any limit and possibility of solvency for people on earth because virtuosity is now determined by the expansion of surplus value.

This compulsion to valorize value is clearly demonstrated by modern charity. When the ultrarich class engages in acts of magnanimity or in grandiose plans to save the world, it does so in ostensible and profitable ways—at a minimum, the investment in charity must grow the brand of the virtuous billionaire, while serving his self-interests.[11] In effect, for the elite, direct access to grace on earth generates two behaviors that are dominated by surplus value: conspicuous opulence—think of the new space craze among oligarchs—and avarice, another of those theological categories that relate to the capitalist unconscious. The miser is the perfect example of somebody driven by the desire of accumulation for accumulation's sake. As Mladen Dolar points out, the miser's wealth becomes the object of all objects, a metaphysic entity or "surplus object" that augments totality not because of some specific goal but because it mirrors infinity. The surplus object is what "in money is more than money, the general equivalent without equivalent."[12] This surplus object is the neoliberal

11. See Anand Giridharadas, *Winners Take All* (Knopf, 2018).
12. Mladen Dolar, "Avatars of Avarice," Jnanapravaha Mumbai Conference, 2019, YouTube video, https://youtu.be/5Uqsgns8h90.

God of Christianity: the creed that demands infinite valorization through extractive practices and debt economy. The miser and their ostentatious opposite display a mimetic behavior. They follow an imaginary Other that is leading us to extinction.

By structuring itself around a transcendent Other that demands the endless expansion of surplus value, neoliberalism not only degrades societies and the ecosystem but also blocks the necessary injection of liquidity to address climate change by invoking the sanctity of the law of payability. Debt is the other side of valorization. Payability is presented as a universal law that, however, does not apply to the economic elite, who always have a path to redemption—we may call a soteriology for the 1 percent. Bailouts are for those who run the financial machine, Dolar points out, as these elites are always granted assistance because they are "in the mercy," eternally saved by virtue of "their very position which entitled them to speculation."[13] As this cast socializes its losses, neoliberal governments staunchly promote the virtuousness of strict austerity measures. The founding principle of this narrative, which Stephanie Kelton has dubbed the "deficit myth," assimilates the household's budget to that of an independent nation.[14] Projected onto the state, this misguided logic demands the slashing of spending to avoid insolvency of future generations. The dark irony is that these fiscal and monetary policies draw their force from a moral argument, the future of our children, precisely when facing the threat of a mass-extinction event. A brief genealogical incursion into the symbolism of money and its meanings will provide insights into how transcendence operates this reversal.

13. Mladen Dolar, "The Quality of Mercy Is Not Strained," *Yearbook of Comparative Literature* 60 (2014): 18.
14. Stephanie Kelton, *The Deficit Myth* (Public Affairs, 2020).

Origin and Meaning of Money

Under capitalism, money, writes Marx, is "the alienated ability of mankind."[15] This process of alienation culminates in the definition of what is essential to this ideology: surplus value, a transcendent infinity that effectively captures excess. In this respect, transcendence forces on society a logic of endless payability as the duty of the individual morphs into a restitution that mirrors infinite growth. Societal needs, in turn, are secondary and must be kept to a bare minimum, just enough to fuel growth. Scott Ferguson has pointed out that capitalism fights against the economic potential of a society—he calls it the "social ontology of money"—to undermine the real goal of the monetary function: the expansion and support of life-forms.[16] The task for a viable economy of infinity is to rescind the symbolic obligations established by the pecuniary version of the Other to fully activate the social ontology of money. To do so, I propose a symbolic genealogy of money inspired by the modern monetary theory school.

Two assumptions ground an intuitive understanding of money. The first is that its value is based on the fact that money is precious—according to this view, all money is a commodity like gold. The second regards the "who" that ultimately guarantees its usage, that is, the relationship with some form of alterity. Let us begin by interrogating the first assumption. History is full of

15. Karl Marx, "Economic and Philosophic Manuscripts of 1844," Marxists Internet Archive, https://www.marxists.org/archive/marx/works/1844/manuscripts/power.htm.

16. Modern monetary theory (MMT) understands money as both credit and fiat money, that is, money made by governmental decree. From this integration, MMT constructs an alternative to austerity focusing on the underutilization of public resources, the only real limit of which is inflation.

examples of societies that do not define money through some intrinsic value, be that utility, beauty, exceptionality, or even scarcity, as in the case of gold. The palatial economy of ancient Tigris and Euphrates societies (where clay tablets functioned as real money) is a case in point.[17] Closer to us in time, Middle Ages authorities periodically retrieved coins from circulation and reintroduced them by determining a new value, an act known as *valor impositus*.[18] Ernst Wolfgang writes that "the circulation of coins was often limited to a statutory period (typically a year), at the end of which all coins had to be returned to the mint."[19] Commonly known as *renovatio monete,* this practice suggests that "money was a matter collectively engineered to entail value anchored by its use in a polity" and not so much in a metallic referent.[20] Historically, *renovatio monete* signals the centrality of politics as well as the emergence of a nonreferential understanding of value. From a political perspective, the royal decision has the last word on the thing of money, while from an economic perspective, the reduction of finesse did not trigger automatic devaluation insofar as liquidity was ensured within the polity.[21]

17. See Michael Hudson, "The Archeology of Money: Debt Versus Barter Theories of Money's Origins," in *Credit and State Theories of Money: The Contributions of A. Mitchell Innes,* ed. L. Randall Wray, 99–127 (Edward Elgar, 2004).

18. See Fabian Wittreck, "Money in Medieval Philosophy," in *Money in the Western Legal Tradition,* ed. David Fox and Wolfgang Ernst (Oxford University Press, 2016), 58.

19. Wolfgang Ernst, "The Legists' Doctrines on Money and the Law from the Eleventh to Fifteenth Centuries," in Fox and Ernst, *Money in the Western Legal Tradition,* 113.

20. Caterina Desan, "Money as a Legal Institution," in Fox and Ernst, *Money in the Western Legal Tradition,* 28.

21. See Alfred Mitchell Innes, "What Is Money?," in Wray, *Credit and State Theories of Money,* 15, and Ernst, "Legists' Doctrines on Money," 113.

If the content of money does not depend simply on a precious metal, or, differently put, if such dependence does not rely on something concrete, it perhaps involves some form of symbolic reference. Consider the case of the gold ingot. One of the safest assets during a crisis, it still necessitates trust in some Other who will accept the lump of metal as payment. Gold objectifies the belief that some Other will redeem that piece of metal by offering something of equal value in exchange. This unspoken agreement points to the way in which money is conditioned by a transcendent dimension that determines its operability. Georg Simmel gestured to this form of abstract obligation in his famous work *The Philosophy of Money*. Published in 1900, this text lays out one of the first important sociological-philosophical studies of money as a noncommodity. One of the key assumptions is the centrality of the notion of trust—Simmel calls it the "supratheoretical belief" in the idea "that the community will assure the validity of the tokens for which we have exchanged the products of our labor in an exchange against material goods."[22] This supratheoretical belief embodies the ontogenesis of money because it lays out the twofold foundation of money. "To believe in someone" means that a community trusts that money will both be accepted as a unit of exchange and retain its worth in time, that is, that it will function as a storage of value. Both elements point to the role of transcendence, a role that is amplified when considering money's capacity to reflect reality in its past, present, and future states. In sum, Simmel observes, money is "the clearest embodiment of the formula of all being."[23] Such capacity to translate any material object into a unit of value sets the stage

22. Georg Simmel, *The Philosophy of Money* (Routledge, 2004), 178.
23. Simmel, 127.

for an understanding of economy as a theological enterprise. Transcendence is first affirmed as the trust in some Other, who will redeem the currency, and successively in an infinite substance: God. While Simmel's insistence on the importance of the trust in the Other demystifies the definition of a currency as commodity money (gold, silver, etc.), it also spiritualizes alterity through a parallel between money and God—insofar as God is an omnipotent totality, money is a universal measure for life.

The problem is not the similitude between money and God— Marx, too, described money as the "object of eminent possession," endowed with the "omnipotence of its being."[24] Rather, Simmel embraces the spiritualized substance of money by positing the market as the matrix of society. "The exchange of the products of labor, or of any other possessions," he writes, "is one of the functions that creates an inner bond between men—a society, in place of a mere collection of individuals."[25] "It is," he concludes, "almost a tautology to say that exchange brings about socialization: for exchange is a form of socialization."[26] From this perspective—one that echoes the classical approach to money by his contemporary Carl Menger—trade, exchange, and barter constitute the nexus of practices that form society. It bears noting that for Simmel, humans have always been businesslike creatures. In paleolithic times, like today, people naturally traded using innate concepts like equivalences, the law of supply and demand, price fluctuation, and so on. Therein the idea of value as exchange price is assumed to be an anthropological fact. In this, Simmel falls in line with an economistic ideology that projects backward and forward a totalizing view of "individuals who have

24. Marx, "Economic and Philosophic Manuscripts."
25. Simmel, *Philosophy of Money,* 174.
26. Simmel, 174.

unlimited desires," which, as Graeber notes, will always create "at least tacit competition."[27] Rather than discovering the origin of sociality, Simmel encounters the point where the economy of infinite valorization meets the economy of rank. Accordingly, the impulse to acquire more (power, wealth, prestige, etc.) is a trait of human evolution just like mimetic rivalry in Girard's economy of rank, where the desire of the Other as the endless expansion of surplus value pushes individuals to compete for status. Infinite valorization is the end point of Simmel's spiritualization of money. Ultimately, he sidesteps the social content of money, what we called the social ontology of money, turning its human origin into an abstract, transcendent force.

In 1905, only five years after the publication of *The Philosophy of Money,* German economist Georg Knapp produced a work that skirts the spiritualization detected in Simmel. In *The State Theory of Money,* Knapp calls autometallism the traditional view that misinterprets the legal and political status of money. "Even in autometallism," he observes, "it is first the possibility of employing [money] in exchange that gives [money] the property of becoming a means of payment." Hence the use of money is, before anything else, "a legal phenomenon."[28] In Knapp's view, moneys are actually nominal debts, that is to say, "debts repayable in the means of payment current at the time."[29] Hence, Knapp concludes, "such nominal debts are not really indefinite. All that is indefinite is the material in which they

27. David Graeber, *Toward an Anthropological Theory of Value* (Palgrave Macmillan, 2001), 257.

28. Georg Friedrich Knapp, *The State Theory of Money* (1905; repr., Martino Publishing, 2013), 6.

29. Knapp, 15.

are discharged."[30] Be it a precious metal or a useful commodity like grain, shells, or even cigarettes, what defines these forms of debt (or IOUs) is their serviceability, the fact that they can transfer to other people.

Knapp's claims regarding serviceability dispel another universal belief about the state. Although common for modern nations, coinage is not essential to the state. The true prerogative of a sovereign state is the power to change the means of payment. This happens not by minting money—historically private institutions oversaw coinage—nor thanks to the market capacity to determine the prices of goods (as in Simmel) but through a political decision on what constitutes an acceptable means of payment. Scholars calls the authorities who make these political decisions "stakeholders." Stakeholders are people, historically councils, vested with symbolic authority. Consider how Christine Desan illustrates the creation of a new unit of account after the disappearance of the monetarized economy in post-Roman England: "The innovation occurred when a stakeholder identified a unit and began to use it as a kind of receipt to represent resources given to the group. . . . One such stakeholder could instead take an amount of goods or services early, giving in return a token that the recipient could provide later at a time of reckoning as proof that the service had been rendered."[31] Stakeholders' role is to mobilize, circulate, and thus guarantee resources for the community. A community thus determines the value of the credits and debts of its transactions. Money is not a private property. The origin and essence of money are always political, as economist Yanis Varoufakis claims.[32]

---

30. Knapp, 16.
31. Desan, "Money as a Legal Institution," 23.
32. Yanis Varoufakis, *Talking to My Daughter About the Economy* (Farrar, Straus, and Giroux, 2019).

To recapitulate my argument so far, transcendence rules by way of symbolic obligations driven by a logic of payability. Money plays a role that, although fundamental, is largely symbolic. Rather than being based on something tangible, money needs a ritualistic act to exist. Simmel focused on the principle of trust in the Other, but this entity quickly loses its social character, turning into the abstraction of the market. Knapp restores the centrality of the political and social dimensions through the role of sovereign authority—that is, stakeholders who validate payment units essential to the circulation of resources; this may lead to coinage, or not, as in post-Roman England. This ambivalence means that money is simply a form of representation of potentialities (resources, work, skills, ideas) that circulate in a community. Money represents the myriad of debts and credits that each member of said group has with one another. What people carry in their pockets are other people's promises of payment. Debts and credits form the incandescent nexus that defines money.

The Currency of the Anthropocene

The Bretton Woods agreement to end gold redeemability did not prevent capitalist ideologues from depoliticizing money. On the contrary, once desubstantialized, autometallism reemerged, imposing a more pernicious tributary bond on the economic discourse. Austerity is the name for that "virtuous" principle that demands that spending be backed by a proportionate revenue stream. In the United States, for instance, the hysteria against the costs of moving toward universal health care or transitioning to a green economy is based on the fear of a deficit that would bankrupt the country. However, recall Knapp's discussion of serviceability. Because a sovereign state is the issuer of the national currency—that is, not just the entity that mints money but also the authority that decides on the means of payment—it does not actually use taxes to fund its operations.[33] Taxes do not create money. The state creates money, which it then redeems via taxes, fines, and other instruments. In this sense, L. Randall Wray argues, "the word redemption is used in two ways: accepting your own IOUs [money] in payment and promising to convert your IOUs to something else," usually "the State's IOUs."[34] The state decides on the resources to service society's needs. But this mobilization must be continually ensured through fiscal operations. As Ferguson writes, "money is not an alienable entity government amasses or hemorrhages. It is a limitless writing instrument for mobilizing social production and provisioning the public purpose."[35] To follow this metaphor, the revenue system is a curator; it guarantees the legibility of this writing by ritualistically taking currency out and back into circulation. This is why there is, Ferguson concludes, "perpetual redemption at the center of money's spiraling temporality."[36] Salvation does not expect us in the afterlife, nor is it something a transcendent entity will grant us. Salvation is the immanent process that nourishes social reproduction.

Transcendence impresses a teleological mark on the progression of time by setting salvation as an end point in one's life and now, under neoliberalism, by substituting redemption with the endless work of restitution. The problem is not the Other but

33. L. Randall Wray, introduction to *Credit and State Theories of Money,* 8.

34. L. Randall Wray, "Modern Money Theory: How I Came to MMT and What I Include in MMT," *New Economic Perspectives* (blog), October 1, 2018, https://neweconomicperspectives.org/2018/10/modern -money-theory-how-i-came-to-mmt-and-what-i-include-in-mmt.html.

35. Scott Ferguson, *Declarations of Dependence* (University of Nebraska Press, 2018), 63. For MMT, the only real internal limit is inflation.

36. Ferguson, 63.

the relation we imagine having with this alterity. The Jubilee complied with this sacred function by alleviating a structural problem in the ancient world. Facing a planetary collapse, the neoliberal response instead ranges from outright denial to inadequate promises, which are always geared toward surplus value. Consider how at the onset of the Russian invasion of Ukraine in 2022 it was predicted that the West would transition faster toward renewables to avoid Russian energy imports. Naturally, the opposite happened. Security concerns and record profits for fossil fuel companies prompted massive investments into new oil and gas projects that will doom any hope of meeting the Paris agreement to limit global warming to below 1.5 degrees Celsius. Governments committed to fighting climate change enacted these policies because, as Timothy Morton writes, neoliberalism can always explain away the costs of externalities and ecological destruction; after all, both capital and nature "exist in an ethereal beyond" capable of absorbing anything.[37] This repression of the ecological boundaries also fuels the discourse of austerity. The logic of payability dominates the political discourse over the ecological and social needs of our societies by setting up an imaginary future of fiscal deliverance, while the true biosocial damages of our present model of production are displaced. Neoliberalism sets up a convenient inverted image: Nature is endlessly manipulable, while the public circulation of money is constrained by transcendence, the great debt collector, which invariably vanishes when military spending knocks on the door.

We need to move away from a symbolic model that represses the alterity we inhabit by projecting it onto the sphere of an Other who desires always more. The task is to sketch an economy of infinity that reflects Virno's economy of noncoincidence at a

37. Timothy Morton, *Hyperobjects* (University of Minnesota Press, 2013), 115.

monetary level, where the otherness of life takes up a political role. To do so, I analyze the new political economy imagined by Robinson's novel *The Ministry for the Future,* which draws on Delton Chen's idea of the Global Carbon Reward. The utopian dimension of this proposal is evident. But the novel's attempt to bring alterity and its infinities into the fold of the social dimension of our present allows us to peer into the possibilities of what I call a *social immanentization of infinity,* that is, a world-forming and life-sustaining infinity detached from surplus value.

Beginning in the mid-2020s, *The Ministry for the Future* maps how a global movement, aided by an unconventional team of bureaucrats, embraces a revolution that includes the rights and voices of the *future* in today's politics. The center of this transformation is a political institution—the ministry that gives the title to the novel—that is charged with the mission of advocating "for the world's future generations of citizens, whose rights . . . are as valid as our own," including "all living creatures present and future who cannot speak for themselves."[38] The Ministry complies with this function not only via legal means but also by promoting and financing initiatives that fight climate change. The office is held by a combative politician, "Mary Murphy, an Irish woman of about forty-five years of age, ex-minister of foreign affairs in the Government of the Irish Republic, and before that a union lawyer."[39] Mary and her international cabinet members are the coprotagonists of the polyphonic and multiform movement that

38. Kim Stanley Robinson, *The Ministry for the Future* (Orbit, 2020), 16.

39. Robinson, 18. Mary resembles another of Robinson's heroes from the Mars Trilogy, Tatiana Durova, an engineer, who similarly directs revolutionary change through institutional means. On the socio-political framework for the trilogy, see Kenneth Knoespel, "Reading and Revolution on the Horizon of Myth and History: Kim Stanley Robinson's Mars Trilogy," *Configurations* 20, no. 1 (2012): 109–36.

culminates in the revolution of 2048. I will say more about this event later on. For now, it is important to take stock of the theoretical principle behind the novel. Through the Ministry, future generations become a stakeholder in today's politics. This alterity finds a form of political representation different from the cultic belief heralded by neoliberalism—the veneration not of the transcendent Other but of the infinities of human generations. This different other is already here and needs care and tending.

The Ministry for the Future stages an epistemological shift in the role and actions of the Ministry that deviates from standard thinking about time. The Ministry functions like a time device that embodies the new temporality of the Anthropocene. Our Newtonian understanding of time states that the future does not exist. However, Robinson attempts to capture a political structure that roots itself in the idea of the immanence of time. Folding the social infinities into the present means bending time, drawing it into the closeness of immanence. The novel illustrates this form of temporal immanence in at least two ways. The first is a paradigmatic shift. Robinson understands environmental change not so much as a near-future possibility but as something that has already happened. Climate change reveals how reality is, in fact, an ensemble of hyperobjects. A *hyperobject* is a category of things, Morton argues, endowed with a dimensionality that liquidates terms like Nature or the World, which is imagined as a transcendent entity, an empty container that is self-standing. Morton argues that "there is no top object that gives all objects value and meaning, and no bottom object to which they can be reduced."[40] Because of their limitlessness, hyperobjects demand a different understanding of time. It is well known that our actions (or inactions) will have a lasting impact on the life-forms that

40. Morton, *Hyperobjects,* 116.

will populate this planet.[41] The fact that the future is embedded in our present forces upon us what Morton calls an "intimacy" with the other.[42] Notice how this contiguity with alterity reflects the economy of noncoincidence of part 1. Recall Virno's remark regarding the deep grammar of the verb *to have*. One could say that we "have" a future because we are in an extrinsic relation of proximity and nonidentity with it, not in one of smooth control. Contrary to that, neoliberalism "is" the future because it identifies with it; it is simply growth.

The second form of temporal immanence emerges within the mottled temporality of the novel itself, which is based on events that disrupt the sameness of neoliberal time. Naturally, the ecological catastrophe structures the timeline of these events as the Ministry becomes a kind of shadow directorate for the green revolution. But the rugged road that leads to this transformation emerges in bursts of historical energy. Sometimes there are bloody spikes, as in large-scale attacks by ecoterrorists against the aviation and fossil fuel industries; at other times, there are more targeted actions, such as sabotages, strikes, and the hilarious *contrapasso*-like punishment whereby a number of CEOs are forced to attend reeducation camps, watching endless PowerPoint presentations on human-induced effects on climate. Geopolitical change takes place as well, mostly from the South of the world—India, Africa, and so on. This turmoil and the catastrophic crescendo culminate in a new Springtime of the Peoples

41. Morton summarizes the unusual temporality of the Anthropocene as follows: "The very large finitude of hyperobjects forces humans to coexist with a strange future, a future without us," given that events like "plutonium and global warming have amortization rates of 24,100 and 100,000 years respectively" (94).

42. Morton, 95.

of 1848. Significantly, what inaugurates this momentous year is a fiscal strike by the National Student's Union in the United States.

> Student debt was a trillion-dollar annual income stream for the banks, so this coordinated default meant that the banks were suddenly in cash-flow hell. . . . This fiscal strike threw them immediately into a liquidity crisis reminiscent of the 2008 and 2020 and 2034 crashes, except this time people had defaulted on purpose, and precisely to bring the banks down. . . . But this time the Fed asked Congress to authorize their bailing out the banks in exchange for ownership shares in every bank that took the offer.[43]

This lucky conjuncture of history whereby the US Congress does the right thing inverts the symbolic mechanism of redemption by eliminating eternal salvation for the elite. It also disrupts the teleology of the debt economy ingrained in such structure because redemption returns to the core of the government's authority not as a shield of an oligopoly but as instrument for the mobilization of the social ontology aimed at the benefit of present and future people. A growing interconnectedness based on this new sense of time animates the spirit of 2048. From a theoretical point of view, this also means that the logic of social reproduction displaces surplus value both as the object of objects and as the discourse of payability. I already observed that because it is infinite, the work of reproduction points to a form of eternity. This timeless dimension thus stretches out toward the future as well, asserting its presence. Whereas the high finance of capitalism claims to predict the future when it only wants to dominate it, Robinson's efforts go in the opposite direction. To safeguard the alterity of the future, humanity devises solutions to protect the ecosystem that nourish the reproduction of relations of humanity and its many others—that is, the alterities I discussed in part 1.

43. Robinson, *Ministry for the Future,* 375.

Money for Social Infinity

The Ministry for the Future directly critiques the two mechanisms that sustain the discourse of transcendence: grace as a teleological direction of time and surplus value as the top object that harnesses life. If the Ministry is the institutional tool that incorporates a new sense of time, money is the second narrative innovation that ends the model of redemption as we know it.[44] As rising levels of CO_2 bring forth unbearable environmental pressures, unprecedented losses and financial exposure for insurance companies provoke a massive crisis of trust in the US dollar.[45] The scale of the devastation opens a fissure in the system by bringing onto the scene the problem of infinity and its economic quantification. This type of infinity is the spiritual driver not of surplus value but of human life. If money is the general equivalent that measures the value of things, these calamities defy standard risk assessment because the cost of remediation inhibits calculation: "So just call it infinity," states Dick Bosworth, the Australian adviser to the Ministry.[46] The issue of representability emerges here as a productive paradox because it inserts itself into the discourse of payability exploding the pactional cage of neoliberalism. Just like with temporality, the novel operates an immanentization of infinity by recognizing its social character.

Standard expansionary fiscal policies are not enough to match the scale of the multiple crises. To finance the mobilization

44. Contrary to the sci-fi genre, Robinson's treatment of money, too, follows an immanent approach, for as Maxximilian Seijo writes, "*Ministry* stays put, prioritizes place, and redefines the money animating our world." Seijo, "Money's Place: Science Fiction, Realism and Modern Monetary Theory in Kim Stanley Robinson's *The Ministry for the Future*," *Money on the Left* 1, no. 1 (2023): 19.

45. Seijo, 54.

46. Seijo, 55.

needed to comply with what Bosworth called "infinity," another form of infinity is needed. Robinson imagines the adoption of a new money, a digital currency explicitly modeled on the Global Carbon Reward Initiative—an actual policy framework developed by Delton Chen. This approach intends to create a parallel economy that would rebalance the carbon cycle as a kind of economic photosynthesis.[47] Under the new reward-base system, various private and public actors who sequester carbon (and are certified by appointed public agencies) are reimbursed with digital credits. Before I turn to the role of the carbon coin, it is important to note that Chen's framework for a carbon reward in effect mimics the infinity of transcendence—the bioremediation work needed to restore acceptable environmental conditions is monumental, although not unlimited, and this is why he sets the unit of account for one coin at one thousand kilograms of CO_2 mitigated for a hundred-year duration.[48] Yet, this amount is shaped not as a limit but as a floor that allows for a proliferation of new initiatives. Robinson's decision to include this monetary innovation in the novel is defamiliarizing in multiple ways. It is not a prophecy nor a prediction but an idea emerging from a looped temporality—one again in line with the Anthropocene—that from the future returns to the past determining it. Furthermore, it offers a counternarrative to the current anarchocapitalist discourse. Ultimately, the carbon coin is a counter bitcoin, not a financial asset but a collective monetary tool "to invest in survival, to go long on civilization."[49]

47. See the Global Carbon Reward Initiative, https:// globalcarbonreward.org/americas-tour-2022/pricing-nature-yale -podcast/.

48. See *Pricing Nature* podcast, Global Carbon Reward Initiative, https://globalcarbonreward.org/carbon-currency/.

49. Robinson, *Ministry for the Future,* 288.

Just like a regular digital currency, in the novel, the carbon coin encompasses all three basic monetary functions of a currency: unit of account, storage of value, and medium of exchange (Robinson imagines the creation of fractions of a carbon coin for daily expenditure called *carboni*).[50] However, because the exchange rate for the carbon coin is set at a level that meets the mitigation target established by the international community, the yield is constantly raising. In this way, the rift between finiteness of the present and infinity of the future is inhibited. Infinity is already present in the empiric world of humans; it inhabits the work of reproduction of social relations. But the nurturing of the material and immaterial needs a proper conduit for that to live. The carbon coin becomes this conduit, an economic policy that avoids relapsing into a new form of adulation of transcendence because its purpose is ensuring a livable ecosphere for the reproduction of social ontology.

The biosphere finally acquires its true value, or as Dick Bosworth summarizes, "its worth to people [becomes] a kind of existential infinity. Gauging the price of saving the biosphere's functions against the cost of losing them would therefore always be impossible."[51] Under this arrangement, a reward, or shall I say redemption, is finally assigned to those who work for the preservation of this life, not the celestial one. This economic revolution deals the final blow to the status quo as the vast majority of people see neoliberal discourse for what it really is: "a kind of existential assumption, as if civilization were a kind of cancer and them all therefore committed to growth as their particular deadly form of life. But this time, growth might be

---

50. Robinson, 356–57. Chen's proposal envisions the Global Carbon Reward as a financial asset, not as a medium of exchange.

51. Robinson, 344.

reconfiguring itself as the growth of some kind of safety."[52] At this point, life is oriented not toward transcendence but toward its own immanent reproduction. Grafted on a series of massive events and violent struggles, the Ministry's push for the carbon coin is the economic platform that unites people in a collective task. It is an economic device in the highest sense: It provides both a symbolic and a material structure for the reproduction of subjectivity and its ecosystem. Social ontology is what anchors Robinson's notion of value and is also why Chen's monetary proposal is so appealing to him. Robinson's understanding of value is economic but not economistic. Capitalism follows an idealized market-based notion of value, the competition for scarce resources that produces profit. The new value for the Anthropocene is the preservation of the other (the many others that form the biosphere) as an immanent form of life. Robinson describes it as a new gold standard, one whereby finance provisions the social and biological basis of life and whose value is defined not by the scarcity of a valuable good that can be hoarded but by the infinite task of mending and nourishing life.

52. Robinson, 345.

3. A Phallic Economy of Time

IN KEEPING WITH AN ECONOMY OF NONCOINCIDENCE, an economy of social infinity includes the prospect of a type of infinity that emerges from our own livelihood. Within it, otherness lives in proximity to us because it is brought into the fold of life—a principle encapsulated by the future generations of *The Ministry for the Future,* who turn into stakeholders of society. Because alterity is an immersive relationship that grows in a zone of contiguity with us, this type of otherness is different from salvation. The carbon coin, for instance, signals the possibility of what Ferguson called a "perpetual redemption," which dissolves salvation and its corresponding logic of payability. Finally, to the extent that it escapes a soteriology, this type of redemption does not structure time teleologically. This conclusion, however, raises the question of how to think time, not just the time of theology but also that of modern society. Neoliberal temporality is not immune from such questioning. On the basis of simultaneity and contemporaneity, neoliberal time measures the intensification of the rhythms of extraction of surplus value, which mobilize individuals through moral and fiscal imperatives. This is the third economy of transcendence, namely, a phallic economy of time.

Whereas the economy of rank targets individuals by imposing templates of rivalry and sacrifice and the economy of infinite valorization represses the natural and human limits unleashing the dictum of austerity—which prevents necessary investments in remediation, carbon reduction, and the global rebuilding of the social infrastructure—the phallic economy of time conceptualizes life as inexorable destruction.[1] Common sense, too, depicts time in such a grim light, for as temporal creatures marked by growth, decay, and death, we normally picture time as an absolute universal order following a fixed direction. There are, however, logical issues with notions like beginning and end that circumscribe life (including that of the universe) that we normally take for granted. Specifically, questions regarding what was there before time—which perhaps caused it to exist—and what will be there after its end point, pointing toward a concept of time limited by, but also based on, external conditions. From this perspective, time, too, is something that comes from nothing and returns to it. This nihilistic conceptualization of time, I argue, is part and parcel of a system of power that is dooming us to extinction. This is why I want to look at how the complexities of immanent infinity can be understood from a temporal point of view by parsing over two interrelated concepts, *Appearing* and *glory,* elaborated by Hannah Arendt and Adriana Cavarero and by an unlikely companion to feminist theory, Emanuele Severino. This dialogue outlines the tenets of an alternative economy of eternity.

Of Matricides and Patricides

As observed, the temporal scale of climate change is so great that it escapes our cognitive capacities. Transcendence offers shelter against this notion of time by establishing a mechanism that reg-

1. I borrow this term from Luce Irigarary's *Speculum of the Other Woman* (Cornell University Press, 1985), 245.

ulates temporal vastity by circumscribing it or, better, by shooting it through with the presumed emergence of nothingness: that which preexisted the beginning, that which will save us from death, or, if you don't believe in the afterlife, the nothingness into which we all turn sooner or later. In Western thought, this conceptualization of time originates with Eleatic philosophy. It is the result of a separation between the corruptible reality of earth and the superior and abstract world of transcendence. Adriana Cavarero writes that in Parmenides, we encounter a philosopher who "abandons the world of his own birth in order to establish his abode in pure thought, thus carrying out a symbolic matricide in the erasure of his birth."[2] An otherworldly being becomes the realm of truth because it persists eternally in its immutable essence, while the becoming-other of the physical world brings into existence nothingness or nonbeing. Here the problem is not so much transformation and multiplicity as it is death, because, Cavarero argues, this is where "nothingness, into which *what is* finally disappears, manifests itself as the destination of becoming, and at the same time as its substance."[3] Cavarero is quick to notice that Plato's famous patricide of Parmenides, which introduces the idea of difference to save reality from annihilation, is only an apparent solution because it is based on a split between the sensorial and illusory dimension of life and the true and universal realm of ideas. In conclusion, "the disavowal of the world's reality in the name of Parmenides' not-being continues to exert its power."[4] By so doing, Western philosophy takes up a nihilistic stance that, by devaluing reality, also makes

---

2. Adriana Cavarero, *In Spite of Plato: A Feminist Rewriting of Ancient Philosophy* (Routledge, 1995), 38.

3. Cavarero, 44.

4. Cavarero, 43.

it expendable or cheap, as Jason Moore calls it.[5] We will see how this conceptualization is the result of symbolic matricide, that is, a continuous disavowal of the form of life we inhabit—this worldview understands birth as the coming-into-being of something from nothing. That nothing, which philosophy needs to understand the concept of origin as creation *ex nihilo,* is, in fact, the persistent gesture of erasure of the mother.

To gauge the effects that this belief in nothingness has on time, let us turn to the philosophy of Emanuele Severino, particularly to his analysis of what he calls the three great discourses of Western civilization: myth, philosophy, and *technē* (technology). This periodization begins with a mythologeme, common to all ancient tales, that perceives becoming as a marker of destruction. Severino writes that to shield themselves from death, "primitive people find a way to coexist with the defunct by considering it another mode of being alive. To those who survived, the corpse has the appearance of that which has been subtracted from the visible."[6] The mythical relationship with death is based on a form of permanence of all that exists; what changes is its visibility. The dead are still with us; they are just less visible. They are spirits. In the myth of Chronos, for instance, the father of the gods does not put an end to his children by eating them, because he vomits them right back into the world so that they keep on living.[7] However, even this type of nonfinal death produces suffering, which, in turn, requires a response in the guise of some saving mechanism. The story of Genesis updates the mythical template by attesting to how mankind attempted (unsuccess-

---

5. Jason Moore, "The Rise of Cheap Nature," in *Anthropocene or Capitalocene?,* 78–115 (PM Press, 2016).

6. Emanuele Severino, *In viaggio con Leopardi: La partita sul destino dell'uomo* (Rizzoli, 2015), 62.

7. See Emanuele Severino, *Il muro di pietra* (Rizzoli, 2006), 19–22.

fully) to defeat God. Adam's and Eve's eating of the apple is an example of divine cannibalism, which signals the will to replace God. But this effort fails. Hence, Severino writes, "after having killed the divine in order to live, mankind is urged to strike up an alliance with God so as to find a remedy against the anguish of death." At this point, mankind begins to imagine transcendence "as the supreme power . . . as the dimension where everything must return to find salvation from death and its anguish."[8] The divine beyond turns into the substance that guarantees permanence and thus offers relief from the transformation of reality into nothing.

Philosophy marks a shift from mythical thinking because it formulates the doubt about the credibility of the ancestral belief in persistence—this is the second moment of Severino's periodization, which begins with early Greek civilization and ends with Hegel. The discourse of philosophy consists in understanding and thus assuming the full power of becoming via a series of different intellectual structures or epistemologies that explain and thus control how reality mutates.[9] Modern epistemologies embrace the idea that "the beings of the world (wholly or in part, all or some aspect of them) issue from and return to Nothing—passing from their nothingness to being a not-Nothing and vice-versa." Hence, Severino concludes, "the supreme evidence of Western civilization consists in the purest and most abysmal alienation—the conviction that Being is nothing."[10] There are different degrees to which this belief is held, but at its core, ni-

8. Severino, *In viaggio con Leopardi,* 63.
9. Severino writes that this trait is already manifest in Aeschylus, who "thinks that truth is the supreme remedy against suffering, anguish, and death." Emanuele Severino, *Il mio ricordo degli eterni* (Rizzoli, 2011), 121.
10. Emanuele Severino, *The Essence of Nihilism* (Verso, 2016), 276.

hilism proves to be the shared foundation for Western thought. All monotheistic religions follow the general template of this form of knowledge. Professing the eternity of the soul and the belief in the afterlife, Christianity, for instance, is firmly rooted in Greek epistemology because it believes in a depreciated version of this world. God is said to have created the world *ex nihilo*. Creation, thus, becomes the locus of transition from being to nonbeing; it is the domain where things disintegrate. For Severino, philosophy capitalizes on the idea that something is and, at a certain point, ceases to be. Fully immersing itself in the transformation of things, the age of philosophy wants to control and direct the process of things' becoming-other (i.e., annihilation). In effect, divine perfection raises problems in the earthly domain because it precludes any possibility for human transformative intervention in it. For humanity to act and dominate the world, divine omnipotence must vacate that world and relinquish its omnipotence.[11] This is why Severino maintains that "the void of nothingness is necessary to becoming, that is, to the supreme evidence of creativity . . . hence there cannot exist any immutable entity filling that void with its presence."[12] The belief in embracing the annihilating truth of becoming (the nonbeing of being) offers the only protection against the ancestral dread of death.

At this juncture, technology takes over philosophy by producing a new discourse that subsumes both myth and philosophy, while embracing the open-ended nature of becoming. Modern

---

11. The actual infinity of God overflows space and time, reducing reality to the domain where the simple mechanical execution of his will occurs. Hence, Severino writes, "from the Christian God one cannot pull the knowledge of a single breadcrumb because if one eliminates God's awareness of it, that breadcrumb ceases to exist." Emanuele Severino, "Le radici del nichilismo: Una questione aperta tra metafisica Cristiana e modernità," *Divus Thomas* 100, no. 3 (1997): 97.

12. Emanuele Severino, *Immortalità e destino* (Rizzoli, 2006), 13.

technology claims the status of God and demands to preside over creativity and the transformation of the world. It does so by erasing God's overdetermining knowledge and replacing it with the full mobilization of reality. Technology declares that "any existing limit (or law) is only factual, historical, provisional, and contingent" and that its apparatus "can and must extend its dominion over things indefinitely" and deploy "its capacity . . . to avert death."[13] As an impersonal will to transform, dominate, and thus alienate reality, *technē* now rules the world by drawing on scientific potentiation. Severino's critique of the discourse of the West is too vast to summarize here, particularly his critique of nonbeing on the basis of logics. Suffice it to say that Severino discloses the inconsistency of hypermodern society, which seems to believe that only a higher dose of nonbeing will save us from nonbeing.

There are alternatives to this thanatological scenario. For Severino, eclipsing nihilism means contemplating the idea that beings are eternal—an idea that can be further explained by feminist thought. The case of the trace can help us better understand Severino's idea of time and movement according to what he calls the structure of Appearing. A trace expresses not the nothingness of a particular thing but rather its disappearance, the fact that something is not visible any longer. Something may be a trace of the past without attesting its dissolution. Through examination, recollection, or simply autonomously, as in the case of an ancient ruin, the past presents itself and reappears. Naturally, as it manifests in its particularity, the memory of an event is not the whole of that event. As Alessandro Carrera writes, "what is never gone and remains 'missing' in the present and out of our hands, is precisely the 'unpastness' of the past . . . which is entirely hidden

13. Severino, 13, 14.

from us for the simple reason that we can only interpret as 'past' the signs the past sends us through its monuments."[14] When applied to the future, this example is more intuitive: a trace of the future is something that, although not appearing, has already a certain undeniable wholeness to it. We should think of the multiplicities of eternal beings analogously to how we perceive the future, something that is not yet visible but that keeps on coming. In effect, anything that appears, even in the present, must do so through a partial image, while that very partiality must also be tied to a totality. Past and future are traces of totality. According to Severino, what we perceive as the passing of time is simply the appearing and disappearing of a portion of reality that exists as a landscape of instants beyond time.

Appearing Is an Immanent Scene

Diffusing the trap of death as nonbeing is crucial for an understanding of time that does not contribute to the devaluation of the world and its consequent exhaustion. However, construing becoming as the movement of appearing and disappearing of a thing is equally problematic. In Western thought, appearances are notoriously inaccurate, whereas truth is imagined as a solid thing that exists beyond exterior manifestations. But isn't the split between a transcendent eternal being (i.e., truth, God, etc.) and the world (i.e., becoming as the nonbeing of matter) precisely what inaugurates the nihilism of Western discourse? To clarify this point, we need to turn to Hannah Arendt and her insistence on the phenomenality of the world, which we should read as a commitment to demystifying any transcendent position or, to

14. Alessandro Carrera, "Every Child Is a Severino Scholar: The Stubborn Persistence of the Past and the Contradiction of Being Born in Time," *Eternity and Contradiction* 4, no. 7 (2022): 65.

use wording more in tune with her conceptual vocabulary, any "source that stands outside history."[15]

Arendt's *The Life of the Mind* begins with this lapidary sentence: "Being and Appearing coincide," a maxim that resonates with Severino's analysis. Although couched in a common understanding of life as death and becoming, the basis for an idea of being that cannot include its absolute negation emerges precisely through what Arendt calls "appearingness."[16] Arendt notes that the superior truth that lies behind exterior manifestations "is conceived only as another appearance" because "our mental apparatus," ultimately, "remains geared to Appearance. The mind, no less than the senses, in its search . . . expects that something will appear to it."[17] The ontological quality of appearingness allows Arendt to deploy a lexicon that avoids *nonbeing,* thus conceiving of birth and death as movements in and out from the scene of the world: "We are of the world and not merely in it; we, too," she glosses, "are appearances by virtue of arriving or departing, of appearing and disappearing."[18] Other indications regarding the continuity of existence emerge when she considers the difference between the absolute time of Newtonian physics and the natural time of the world, where "the world has neither *beginning* nor *end,* an assumption," she concludes, "that seems only natural for beings who always come into a world that preceded them and will survive them."[19] The propensity for positive determinations offered by the point of view of birth produces an overflowing that constantly appears (rather than freezing) on the

15. Dean Hammer, "Hannah Arendt and Roman Political Thought: The Practice of Theory," *Political Theory* 30, no. 1 (2022): 128.

16. Hannah Arendt, *The Life of the Mind* (Harcourt, 1978), 19.

17. Arendt, 24.

18. Arendt, 22.

19. Arendt, 21.

horizon. The noun *beginning* corresponds to the gerund form of the verb *to begin.* (A gerund expresses an ongoing action.) To put it simply, beginning is not a singular event but rather perpetuates itself endlessly. To begin is, by nature, to keep beginning.

As in Severino's philosophy, plurality, multiplicity, and eternity are key elements for Arendt's definition of appearingness as a relational configuration. Not surprisingly, Andrew Benjamin argues that the structure of Appearing in Arendt is based on the notion that "Appearing is always that which occurs with others. Thus, Appearing is always relational."[20] Benjamin also clarifies that in addition to relationality and the place, the other characteristic of Appearing is that it is *aboriginal.* There is no *principium,* because Appearing is always emergent. Appearingness is the aboriginal because "it precedes. It precedes in the exact sense that it is an ever-attendant possibility."[21] The reason for this is that only a true discontinuity may mark the initiation of beginning. But this break cannot represent what we usually imagine. In fact, the concept of the beginning of all beginnings is simply modeled after transformations we witness every day: an incessant process that has no origin. In this sense, ontological proofs for the existence of God, such as Thomas Aquinas's argument, simply put a stop to the logical regression by saying that God is the uncreated. By installing a father (not a mother) at the top, the chain of reproduction comes to a halt. But because beginning is rooted in the process of life, which is always plural and feminine, the need of a transcendent origin withers away.

20. Andrew Benjamin, "Being and Appearing," *Arendt Studies* 2 (2018): 224.
21. Benjamin, 223. Similarly, Benjamin notes that "the space of appearance is characterized by a foundational irreducibility." Andrew Benjamin, "Thinking Life: The Force of the Biopolitical," *Crisis Critique* 9, no. 2 (2022): 72.

Arendt articulated the concept of appearingness under the category of political praxis, most famously in *The Human Condition,* in chapters where she considers power, action, and politics in the Greek polis.[22] In this text, we encounter a broader understanding of this structure, which is in tune with her notion of birth as a plurality of beginnings. In the same passage in which she writes that our political life "is like a second birth," she also points to a nonanthropocentric space of appearance. She writes that "the new always happens against the overwhelming odds of statistical laws and their probability. . . . The new therefore always appears in the guise of the miracle."[23] The nascent force of life produces the miracle of actualizations that fall into the sphere of Appearing. The miracle of life does not appear only to humans, nor does life appear to some imaginary divine entity. Appearing happens among the multitudes that populate a place. We have two elements at play here: relations between gazes and a place and the scene as the pure presenting of an open system. This is why appearing always involves the other: "Only the spectator, never the actor, can know and understand whatever offers itself as a spectacle."[24] This theatrical reconfiguration of appearingness bears testimony to how the subject is not in charge, nor does it fully possess its identity. In Arendt, the plurality and multiplicity of the scopic are vivified through the notion of the many others that are part of the scene, while the subject loses its centrality in terms of identity and self-actualization. With Arendt, we begin to perceive a form of time that is emergent and

22. Arendt agrees with St. Augustine, who differentiated the beginning *(initium)* of human life from creation *(principium),* that is, the beginning of the world. See Hannah Arendt, *The Human Condition* (University of Chicago Press, 2018), 350n3.

23. Arendt, 157–58.

24. Arendt, *Life of the Mind,* 92.

immanent. Using Severino's language, phenomenality ultimately means that eternity is appearingness: the appearing of a scene that leaves behind other parts, which in turn may emerge at the expense of others.

What practical use do we have for these considerations regarding the eternal dimension of Appearing? How do they inform our urgent need for political action? The answer for Arendt is to move from the plurality of appearingness to the concept of glory. Drawing on the work of zoologist Adolf Portman, she reformulates appearingness from the standpoint of a biological, or sexed, matrix. It is life's particular tendency to manifest as a scene that strikes Arendt as a profound political idea. She writes, "Whatever can see wants to be seen, whatever can hear calls out to be heard, whatever can touch presents itself to be touched"; in other words, life must "fit itself into the world of appearances by displaying and showing, not its inner self but itself as an individual."[25] Appearingness is thus tied to a necessary sensorial dimension, a staging before others who concur to produce a subjectivity. This subjectivity is different from the (universally male) Cartesian subject. As Cavarero glosses, "the fact that the category of personal identity postulates another as necessary" for somebody to appear "has the merit of exemplifying the reason for which an identity constitutively exposed to others is also unmasterable."[26] The self is a mirror house of gazes. Among dazzling reflections, an authentic individuality emerges as a response to how a selfhood has come to see itself through the eyes of others. Owing to the priority of visibility and the constitutive role of the

25. As Arendt writes, "the criterion for vision is only the quality of everlastingness in the seen object" (139).

26. Adriana Cavarero, *Relating Narratives: Storytelling and Selfhood* (Routledge, 2000), 21.

others for subjectivity, Arendt discovers an alternative option to the secluded contemplation of the high truth pursued by the thinking subject of classic philosophy.[27]

Crucially, the concept of glory culminates the scopic plurality of appearingness. Recall that an economy of rank is rooted in "the pleasure of eminence, of having the superior position with the other who is in awe of me."[28] Therein glory functions as a two-step process that involves the other. The first step is an agonal situation in which the other is constructed as the opponent; the second step, after the hero's victory, forces the other into the role of the spectator who pays homage to the winner. If Arendt's early understanding of glory falls along Girardian lines, Peg Birmingham writes that, later, she called "for a transformed notion of glory, no longer rooted in sovereign, sacrificial violence, but instead, in a conception of political responsibility charged with the task of bearing the world."[29] Great art achieves this kind of glory, according to Arendt. However, this shift gains a relevance that is greater than art once glory is reframed in terms of gender. For the symbolic dimension of men, the worthy (but ultimately obsequious) opponent is ultimately the woman. As Carla Lonzi writes, the role of the woman is of one who "implicitly contrasts the history of his supremacy; since she does not fully impede the latter, she also validates it, enriching it with

27. The phenomenality of the world is already the space for political action she calls *vita activa,* which contrasts Plato's priority assigned to contemplation as "the human activity par excellence," where "to see rather than to act is what . . . renders men human." Adriana Cavarero, "Regarding the Cure," *Qui Parle* 10, no. 1 (1996): 4.

28. Peg Birmingham, "Arendt and Hobbes: Glory, Sacrificial Violence, and the Political Imagination," *Research in Phenomenology* 41, no. 1 (2011): 7.

29. Birmingham, 12.

pathos."[30] This is why we argued that masculine desire is about a symbolic position. This subject never encounters a specific feminine individual but rather encounters a type that conforms (more or less) with the expected agonal entity. Arendt attempts to resignify this masculine characterization of glory. Glory thus becomes the plural space of appearingness that stages the possibility for the endless proliferation of the uniqueness of each individuality. Glory shines in the sensory interplay that takes place in the exposing of a singularity.

In effect, there is a hint of glory in the distinctiveness of every individual being. In *The Human Condition,* for example, Arendt connects plurality and singularity via the notion of action when she says that "plurality is the condition of human action because we are all the same, that is, human, in such a way that nobody is ever the same as anyone else who ever lived, lives, or will live."[31] The singularity of each individuality displaces the masculine attempt to reduce this inner flame to the dark night of sameness. Therein we find a path to the glorious deed. Insofar as individuals and life in general exist to show themselves, glory means to be one with that singular ontological dimension, so that said singularity appears as such to others. This is how Arendt puts it: "Because of its inherent tendency to disclose the agent together with the act, action needs for its full appearance the shining brightness we once called glory, and which is possible only in the public realm."[32] Glory thus entails a communal space of recognition for the deed to emerge. The adherence between the deed and its doer culminates in the brilliance of the scene. Again, I want to stress that this glorious deed is different from a

30. Carla Lonzi, "La donna clitoridea," in *Sputiamo su Hegel* (et al. Edizioni, 2010), 100.

31. Arendt, *Human Condition,* 8.

32. Arendt, 180.

heroic feat fueled by the prodigious will of larger-than-life men. What ignites the flame of glory is the interplay between the doer who reveals herself or himself to the others without completely understanding her or his identity because "the who which appears so clearly and unmistakably to others remains hidden to the person himself."[33] As Alison Martin writes on the glorious scene, "the main protagonist is a doer of deeds but not their author."[34] The communal quality of the scene produces glory.

Taking stock of the centrality of the communal dimension in the concept of glory, we begin to grasp a different kind of social and thus temporal dimension where, as Arendt writes, "people are with others and neither for nor against them—that is, in sheer human togetherness."[35] Plurality and difference characterize this condition together with the liquidation of the pretense of willed intentionality, or the will to dominate reality through processes of creative destruction typical of our societies. This is for Arendt an inherent political trait of life, because "the smallest act in the most limited circumstances bears the seed of the same boundlessness, because one deed, and sometimes one word, suffices to change every constellation."[36] Glory is the appearing of an action that is impersonal, not self-serving, and fully immanent in its extensiveness of the boundless space of the communal. If Severino shed light on the illusions of nihilism reconstructing a transcendental framework for an immanent totality where being and Appearing signify the fullness of eternity, Arendt enriches that totality by including political action and the plurality of the different life-forms of others.

33. Cavarero, *Relating Narratives,* 21.
34. Alison Martin, "Report on 'Natality' in Arendt, Cavarero and Irigaray," *Paragraph* 25, no. 1 (2002): 38.
35. Arendt, *Human Condition,* 180.
36. Arendt, 190.

The Economy of Gazes in a Gendered Eternity

As observed, the nihilistic logic of the West pierces through the continuity of reality by othering it, that is, by assigning not-being to being, a mechanism that impacts our relationships with ourselves and the environment. As illustrated in the case of the agon, one usually finds the woman hidden behind the other both as worthy opponent and tributary entity. In a more constructive vein, Arendt revealed the positive role of others and their world-forming function that defines the idea of glory. I want to conclude by returning to Cavarero to offer a broader elucidation of the temporal fullness of reality from the vantage point of life.

Reflecting on Arendt's idea of visibility, Cavarero notices that "self-showing and reciprocal exhibition" to the other have their roots in the mother, as she is "the other to whom the existent first appears."[37] This is another reason why identity is exposed to the other from the beginning and cannot be completely owned by the subject. This symbolic origin—that is, the beginning that keeps on beginning—is constituted by the child–mother complex. As Luisa Muraro writes, this symbolic structure provides access to language and its immanence, that is to say, "the certainty that words are in relations with being and not with nothing."[38] The maternal order mirrors the structure of Appearing, particularly its world-forming capacity that reverses the discontinuity of male thought by disclosing a permanency that moves backward and forward in time.

37. Cavarero, *Relating Narratives,* 20, 12.
38. Luisa Muraro, "On the Relations Between Words and Things," in *Another Mother: Diotima and the Symbolic Order of Italian Feminism,* ed. Cesare Casarino and Andrea Righi (University of Minnesota Press, 2018), 121.

Cavarero develops the scopic side of this relationship, thus returning the transcendental category of Appearing to the sexed dimension of life: a chain of births as structured through the mother–daughter continuum. She calls this form of visibility the gaze between mother and daughter. Her seminal text *In Spite of Plato* develops this economy of gazes, especially through a rereading of the myth of Demeter. Her analysis unearths the interdicted foundation of Hesiod's *Theogony,* which establishes the agricultural myth of the cycle of the seasons, by demonstrating that Hades's abduction of Demeter's daughter Kore (or Persephone) produces a blockage in the structure of reproduction. In other words, Hades's violence prevents the actualization of the reproductive power lodged in motherhood, signaling a change whereby "death replaced birth as the fundamental paradigm" of the symbolic order—one that "reigned unchallenged in the age of Plato."[39] Referring to the interpretation of this myth by Luce Irigaray, Cavarero adds that this symbolic dimension, "having separated philosophy from embodiedness, being from appearance, . . . turned this dichotomy into the philosophical systems of all systems."[40]

In the myth, the pain of Demeter turns the earth sterile. Only Zeus's intervention saves humans from starvation. The compromise he strikes with Hades inaugurates the agricultural cycle: Kore can return to her mother for part of the year (the fertile periods of spring and summer), while remaining in the underworld for the rest (fall and winter). Cavarero is interested in the crucial role played by vision in this narrative. She notes that because it is "the mother who stops generating when the daughter is snatched out of her sight . . . the maternal power to

39. Cavarero, *In Spite of Plato,* 58.
40. Cavarero, 59.

generate is coextensive with the reciprocal visibility of mother and daughter."[41] The reciprocal gaze is thus the missing link in our journey from the cosmic order of eternity to the earthly dimension of life. It conjoins Arendt's idea of birth and Severino's perspective on the eternity of being(s). The gaze is the pillar for a symbolic dimension that displays the positivity of reality. Naturally, it does so via a partiality. But this partiality does not negate the plural configuration of reality. This is not the image that appears in phallic discourse, which is based on a rhetoric of imposition and distinctiveness guaranteed by symbolic status— quite the opposite. The economy of gaze shows all the elements of Arendt's glory: the symbolic dependency on the other(s); the singularity of the individual, which is granted precisely by various projections of identity that grow out of that dependency; the lack of an essentialized subject who believes that he can possess (and thus destroy) reality; and ultimately, the full consistency of being as an immanent plane.

The mother–daughter continuum is the space where Appearance is directed toward humanity. In Cavarero's phrasing, "the female gender . . . demands that gender itself be a common horizon of recognition for every woman, so that birth, which has already happened, can (but does not have to) happen again."[42] Notice the emphasis on appearance as an emergent structure. As every other organism, the human species is part of the space of appearance. The patriarchal order has foreclosed that filial continuum, thus producing the need for transcendence in the guise of the Father, whose authority usually rests on further forms of transcendence: Truth, Blood, God, and so on. By bringing procreative power into focus instead, we re-

41. Cavarero, 61.
42. Cavarero, 64.

install humankind in the murky infinity of life. In so doing, we also liquidate the problem of becoming as the annihilation of being. There is no creation *ex nihilo,* because we are inhabitants of infinity. In the plane of immanence, Cavarero explains, "the women stage a deployment of prehuman, infinite maternal power, indicating that the divine does not reside in the hierarchical end point of the process of hominization . . . but at the earliest point, at the origin, in the animal innocence that holds onto [*sic*] life without reflection."[43]

Properly decoded, the myth of Demeter illustrates how the famous enigma of not-being is simply the appearing "of nothingness onto the stage as birth-no-more."[44] This form of nothingness is not a thing in itself but a negation of the positivity of the maternal continuum. Nonbeing is simply the inhibition of said continuum. The world lodges "the possibility of stopping the process of regeneration inherent in maternal power" or, as Cavarero explains, "no longer becomes nothingness, a nothingness that is not beyond this world. It is not the nothingness of male philosophers who identify it with death. . . . It is rather the nothingness of birth," because "far from being a coming from nothing, birth is a coming from a mother."[45] In this sense, Severino similarly remarks that the truth of nothingness does not exist, that there is always the truth of something, as in the case of birth-no-more.[46] This is the nothingness that the myth of Demeter reflects: a mythical nonbeing that philosophers fantasize ending up in various illogical dead ends.

43. Cavarero, 112.
44. Cavarero, 60.
45. Cavarero, 61.
46. See Emanuele Severino, "Il destino," posted by Diotima Quattroduetre, October 18, 2013, YouTube video, 21:26, https://youtu.be /KUoh_F8i0bo.

In Plato's *Theaetetus,* however, Cavarero finds a form of speech that "carries within it despite its intentions . . . some type of feminine word that the text itself conveys while failing to comprehend."[47] The anecdote she examines is that of Thales, who, absorbed in his astronomical observation, falls into a well. A young, beautiful maidservant from Thrace laughs at him, declaring that "the things around you, at your feet, are hidden from your sight."[48] As in the case of Parmenides, Thales's philosophy splits being from appearance: Truth resides in the elsewhere of the sky, while the world teems with errors, shadows, and death. No wonder he misses the well. Confronted with the unfortunate accident, the girl's laughter represents not the scorn of the uncultivated person but rather the wisdom that deconstructs the nihilism of Western discourse. By bringing into focus the significance of the phenomenality of the world, the maidservant discloses a metonymic relationship to the world. Recall that the elsewhere of transcendence constitutes reality by submitting it to its universality, which, as I indicated, asserts itself by subjecting every particularity to the sameness of its logic. In contrast, the metonymic chain is built through adjacency of singularly unique elements. The maidservant lapidary sentence flashes this contiguity out: "Things that are *near* you, at your feet." Not the elsewhere of (male) sameness but rather the vicinity of life and its appearances discloses the totality of beings. It is the empirical presence of these singularities that, according to Cavarero, attests to the fact that life "is always gendered" and "renewed at every birth."[49] The maidservant sheds light on Appearing as the logical truth of motherhood.

47. Cavarero, *In Spite of Plato,* 50.
48. Quoted in Cavarero, 56.
49. Cavarero, 55.

As observed, the mother–daughter nexus reveals a fullness in which the new life can be understood only through the relation with the other. This other is the mother (or whoever takes her place). Her symbolic order enables the first form of visibility, which will grow through self-exposition to others. But this economy of gazes is never identical; on the contrary, it lives of and produces uniqueness. This is the glory that comes forth: the singularity of natality.

The father's and mother's symbolic orders are in stark opposition. As Muraro illustrates, the masculine schema is generally hypermetaphorical: It synthesizes everything under the purity and immobility of the idea; that is, it subsumes particularities into sameness.[50] The feminine genealogy instead understands difference as the necessary condition of the movement of the continuum. Severino's move is to bring eternity back into the empiric by way of phenomenality. Naturally, eternity does not denote singular everlasting life. Likewise, the eternal glory of the continuum is not based on some empirical immortality. This form of eternity is logico-symbolical. When it is impossible to cancel out a relationship, as is the case for the idea that everybody is of woman born, these relationships are actually eternal.[51]

50. Luisa Muraro, "To Knit or to Crochet?," in *Another Mother*, 92–93.

51. I borrow this argument from David Graeber, who, speaking about total prestations in Mauss, writes that these relations "between individuals and groups" are "permanent precisely because there [is] no way to cancel them out by a repayment. The demands one side could make on the other were open ended because they were permanent; nothing would be more absurd than for the member of an Iroquois moiety to keep count of how many of the others' dead each had recently buried, to see which was ahead. . . . Most of us treat our closest friends this way. No accounts need be kept because the relation is not treated as if it will ever end." Graeber, *Toward an Anthropological Theory of Value*, 218.

Every birth reenacts in difference the mother–daughter contin-uum. The structure of Appearing has the form and rhythm of a metonymic series.

Natality functions somehow like a trace of past and future events. Unless, of course, the gaze is interrupted, natality al-lows us to touch permanence. Death as the destruction of being or nothingness, in fact, vanishes in an eternal plenitude that looks at the past not as a sequence of deaths but as "an infinite procession of births in reverse."[52] In this sense, the true reme-dy against death resides in the secrets of natality, not as in the patronymic ploy to ensure eternity but in the interconnected composition of gazes of the many glorious scenes each sin-gularity contributed to form. As for the future, here, too, the masculine craves a form of eternity that is misplaced. It is the infinite gestation of life that most closely resembles the virtual-ity of the space of Appearing. As Cavarero glosses, the feminine understanding of Appearing has "no beginning and therefore no nothingness, since the beginning has always initiated, gen-erating both backward and toward infinity, within the horizon (adequate to the observer) that contains it and continues to be repeated and confirmed every time a woman gives birth."[53] Birth as a continuum is the glowing of Appearing. Through the maternal structure, the inherence to the emergent (i.e., the true nature of reality) exposes the collapse of the fantasy of tempo-ral transcendence as both beginning and end. This is a different economy of time based on a type of relationality that connects the eternity of instantaneous scenes, which nobody masters. This is an idea of time that allows for a meaningful relation with

---

52. Cavarero, *In Spite of Plato,* 112.
53. Cavarero, 112.

alterity (based on noncoincidence) and the full appreciation of the life-sustaining capacity of the social infinity we inhabit. The demise of the third pillar of transcendence breaks the fever of a phallic economy of time. Through the smoke of its ruins, one discerns a temporal infinity that values the permanence of endless regenerative relations.

Acknowledgments

This text was partially funded through grants from Miami University. I want to thank colleagues from the French, Italian, and Classical Studies Department for their support and generosity. I also want to express my gratitude to Alessandro Carrera, Michael Lewis, and Scott Fergusson for their commentaries and suggestions.

(Continued from page iii)

Forerunners: Ideas First

Andrea Righi is professor of European languages and Italian at Monash University, Australia. He is the author of *The Other Side of the Digital: The Sacrificial Economy of New Media* (Minnesota, 2021) and *Italian Reactionary Thought and Critical Theory: An Inquiry into Savage Modernities* (2015). He is co-editor of *Another Mother: Diotima and the Symbolic Order of Italian Feminism* (Minnesota, 2018) and *TOTalitarian ARTs: The Visual Arts, Fascism(s) and Mass-Society* (2017).